WRESTLING UNMASKED

Ripping the Mask off the Crime, Politics and Intrigue Beyond the Ring

D1523294

WRESTLETALK
MAGAZINE

CONTENTS

FOREWORD

Oli Davis

When I first heard about "Wrestling Unmasked: Ripping the Mask off the Crime, Politics and Intrigue Beyond the Ring", I thought: "Finally, someone is going to address Retribution's criminal damage of the WWE Performance Center when they smashed that glass door that one time."

Then I was told that was a storyline angle, and the book would actually tackle real behind-the-scenes workings, the backstage drama, and how the dark heart of professional wrestling has very real implications for our day-to-day lives, corporate America, and even how entire nations govern themselves.

I said, that's a much better premise for a book. Retribution's debut would only get you 14-or-so pages.

But this book isn't just a compilation of juicy backstage stories. Who snipped off whose ponytail on a transatlantic flight. No, "Wrestling Unmasked" goes beyond that. It challenges us to look beyond the flamboyance, to not be distracted by crazy backstage politics, to instead confront the real issues that have shaped this most unique of sports. Or arts. Or entertainments.

It's hard to categorise.

Dave Bradshaw's exploration into WWE's dance with politics in "No Holds Barred" is a stark reminder that the wrestling world isn't just about entertainment; it's deeply intertwined with the political landscape, often with consequences.

"Strength in Numbers" delves into the ever-present debate of unionisation in wrestling. With the highly controversial 'independent contractors' status, why haven't wrestlers banded together for their rights?

There's the poignant "Pride and Prejudice", a tribute to Pat Patterson and a hopeful glance at the future for LGBT+ performers and fans in wrestling. It's a testament to the industry's evolving stance on inclusivity.

"The Show Must Go On" takes us back to the aftermath of 9/11, reminding us of WWE's role in America's healing process. Meanwhile, "Middle East Misadventures" and the two-part deep dive into the Chris Benoit tragedy highlight the complexities and challenges wrestling faces on the global stage.

From the industry's relationship with organised crime in "Smoke Without Fire" to the erosion of kayfabe in "Curtain Open", this book promises a journey that's both enlightening and thought-provoking.

So, to all my fellow wrestling fans, I urge you to dive into this book. Challenge your perceptions, reflect on the past, and look forward to the future of wrestling. Because, as "Wrestling Unmasked" shows, the real drama isn't just in the ring; it's in the stories, the people, and the societal issues that shape the sport.

NO HOLDS BARRED: WHEN WRESTLING AND POLITICS COLLIDE

Issue 23, November 2020

Dave Bradshaw

As the 2020 US election campaign reached its final weeks, Dave Bradshaw looked at the history of WWE's interactions with the world of politics - and found that it has not always ended well...

It was supposed to be a fluke. On 4th November 1998 America woke up to the news that Jesse 'The Body' Ventura, the former WWF wrestler and commentator, had scored a shock win in the Minnesota governor's election, defeating both the Republicans and the Democrats in a close three-way race despite trailing in opinion polls throughout the campaign. Branding himself as a straight-talking antidote to the career politicians in both parties, Ventura seemed like a breath of fresh air to many in the state - especially younger voters who supported him in large numbers.

At the time, the reaction from the political establishment and mainstream media was one of ridicule and bemusement - the Washington Post noted that he would be *"the nation's first governor to have his own action figure"* - but the result was otherwise written off by most as an anomaly. After all, it was pretty unlikely that American voters would ever again choose a loud-mouthed celebrity with more experience in professional

1

wrestling than professional politics to represent them in high office... wasn't it?

In hindsight, maybe it was obvious that Ventura's election was part of a growing trend – after all, Ronald Reagan's background as a Hollywood actor suggested that the American public had a soft spot for charismatic performers who were not career politicians. If you think about it, success in wrestling requires plenty of skills that are applicable to the political arena: it's essential to find ways of 'getting over' with the public, it requires a personality that is comfortable being the centre of attention, you need a good catchphrase to make you memorable, and you need to cut devastating promos against your opponents.

In fact, a quick glance across the Pacific Ocean would have indicated that pro wrestlers transitioning to public office was far from ridiculous – by 1998 NJPW founder Antonio Inoki had already carved out a second career for himself in the Japanese Diet (their equivalent of the US Senate or the UK's House of Lords) and, bizarrely, had been directly responsible for securing the release of over a hundred Japanese hostages in Iraq before the first Gulf War when he personally negotiated with Saddam Hussein and agreed to stage a wrestling show in Baghdad as part of the deal. Admittedly, the image of the sport in Japan made it less improbable than in the US that a wrestler would be taken seriously as a politician but still, the fact remained that Inoki had blazed a trail and his peers around the world duly took note.

Fast forward two decades and the list of people connected to the wrestling business who subsequently got involved in politics has gone from a slow trickle to a steady stream. Of course, the most obvious examples are Donald Trump's remarkable rise to the White House and Linda McMahon's two campaigns for a US Senate seat in Connecticut (more on that later), but there are many more examples beyond those two: Glenn 'Kane' Jacobs is currently halfway through his term as the mayor of Knox County, Tennessee; Jerry 'The King' Lawler achieved a respectable share of the votes in two losing efforts to become mayor of his native Memphis in 1999 and 2009; former WWF champion Bob Backlund's unsuccessful run in 2000 for a seat in the US House of Representatives saw him produce several hilarious TV ads that were harshly described by some fans as being better than any promo from his wrestling career; Rick Steiner made national headlines in 2006 when he was disqualified from the ballot for the Cherokee County School Board in Atlanta because his real name is not Rick Steiner (he was subsequently elected later that same year after re-applying with the correct name); B. Brian Blair of the 1980s tag team The Killer Bees was elected as County Commissioner of Hillsborough County, Florida, in 2004; and former ECW World Champion Terrance 'Rhyno' Gerin ran unsuccessfully for the Michigan House of Representatives in 2016. Meanwhile, Inoki protégé and former two-time IWGP Junior Heavyweight Champion Hiroshi Hase became Japan's Minister of Education, Culture, Sports, Science and Technology in 2015 - the highest political office that anyone associated with wrestling anywhere had reached until Donald Trump's victory the following year.

Interestingly, all of the American names listed above either stood for office as a Republican, the more right-wing and conservative of the two main US parties, or have expressed support for its leader Donald Trump in the recent past. Indeed, despite research showing that wrestling's fanbase skews more towards Democrats (the party of Barack Obama and Joe Biden), it seems that the political views of those who work in the business have historically leant heavily to the right. Aside from the names just mentioned, there are plenty of other big names with links to the Republicans. Ric Flair is said to have seriously considered running as the party's candidate for governor of North Carolina in the year 2000 and for a couple of years afterwards, although he was reportedly talked out of it because of the amount of negative stories from his colourful past that might be dredged up if he were to proceed. The 'Nature Boy' has nonetheless offered public support for multiple Republican candidates in elections through the years, including the evangelical Mike Huckabee during his 2008 run for president.

Earlier, WWE Hall of Famers Fritz von Erich and Ernie Ladd had both been influential in Texas Republican politics during their lifetimes, and Ladd enjoyed a close friendship with both Presidents Bush. Commentators JBL and Joey Styles have both been vocal in their support for the Republican party too - in fact Styles got in some trouble in 2009 for calling Barack Obama a "Marxist" on Twitter and criticising the president's "pro-abortion" views, although according to some reports the comments actually endeared Styles to Vince McMahon. Overall, despite the occasional Democrat like Mick Foley putting his head above the proverbial parapet, the culture backstage in WWE through the years seems to have been overwhelmingly Republican. One source told the Wrestling Observer around the time of the Styles controversy that "guys have gotten favoured status based on being outrageously outspoken on being far right" and that the frequent political discussions on McMahon's private jet and in internal company meetings were "always anti-Democrat discussions."

A (MOSTLY) CAUTIOUS APPROACH

Given this apparent company culture, one might expect that there would also have been frequent bias on WWE television during the years, but in fact that is not the case. Although the company undoubtedly takes some stances that are more commonly associated with Republicans - most notably its strong support for the US military, such as during the annual

Tribute to the Troops show - there have scarcely been any overtly partisan messages during the company's history and relatively few storylines or gimmicks that were directly related to current affairs. Of course there are some notable exceptions, none of which is more high profile than the controversial feud between Hulk Hogan and Sgt Slaughter around the time of the first Gulf War. In the autumn of 1990, shortly after Saddam Hussein's Iraq had invaded the neighbouring country of Kuwait, Slaughter returned to the WWF after a lengthy absence and adopted the gimmick of an Iraqi sympathiser, with the company even going so far as to show (fake) photos of him posing with Saddam Hussein. In January 1991, just days after the US and its allies began air assaults in Iraq, Slaughter defeated the Ultimate Warrior at the Royal Rumble to win the WWF Championship and set up a Wrestlemania main event with the ever-patriotic Hulk Hogan.

There was uproar across the country at WWF's perceived exploitation of a real-life conflict to sell tickets for its biggest show of the year: several major newspapers called for letter-writing campaigns to WWF and its sponsors demanding that the storyline be halted, and famous sportscaster Bob Costas pulled out of a celebrity appearance at Mania after deciding it would be in poor taste. What the company thought of all this free (albeit negative) publicity is not clear although they certainly did not shy away from proceeding with the angle for several more months, even though the negative reaction from some fans was arguably part of the reason that WrestleMania had to be moved from the 90,000-seat Los Angeles Memorial Coliseum to the 17,000-capacity Sports Arena. WWE has often claimed in the years since the event that it was moved for security reasons due to death threats to Slaughter, but it is widely believed that poor ticket sales were the main reason.

Perhaps because of this episode, other examples of politically charged angles in WWE are harder to come by. Lex

Luger's nationwide bus tour on the star-spangled Lex Express in the buildup to Summerslam '93 obviously borrowed heavily from political campaigns, but despite this being another example of a flag-waving babyface staring down a foreign menace - this time the enormous Yokozuna - the lack of any current military conflict between the US and Japan made this less provocative than the Slaughter controversy two years earlier, as did the small technical detail that Yokozuna wasn't actually Japanese.

Meanwhile in 1996 a new faction, the Nation of Domination, played into the ever-present racial tensions in the US by mimicking the Nation of Islam and the Black Panthers, while its leader Faarooq (Ron Simmons) cut promos about black talent being held back in the WWF. In one particularly memorable in-ring segment, the supposedly heel Faarooq asked Vince McMahon why there had never been a black world champion in the company. Despite the crowd's relentless booing, there were surely some viewers even back then who wondered if the Nation weren't really the good guys in that situation. Looking back at it in 2020, in the age of Black Lives Matter, it makes for particularly uncomfortable viewing.

In terms of references to specific politicians within WWE programming, the two most notable examples both come from the mid-2000s, and both are really... odd. In December 2006 Cryme Tyme did an in-ring skit with a George W Bush impersonator, which presumably someone somewhere found hilarious: the "president" was introduced as a "character witness" for JTG and Shad Gaspard, and proceeded to defend himself against claims that he didn't like black people by listing his black friends, including saying that his Secretary of State Condoleezza Rice is "one hot little black b****." He then teased saying the N-word before Cryme Tyme stopped him, gave him a hug and stole his wallet to close the segment. Presumably this was all deemed acceptable because weeks earlier when Cryme Tyme had been introduced to the audience via a series of vignettes, each one was preceded by a disclaimer stating that the new tag team would be "parodying racial stereotypes" in an "attempt at Saturday Night Live like humor [that] is bound to entertain audiences of all ethnic derivations." Setting aside issues of taste, it was a parody of Bush that came from out of nowhere, and seemed out of character for a Republican-leaning company that by this time was not known for commenting on party politics.

The second such incident happened sixteen months later, when at least the timing made more sense given that the US was deep into a historic presidential election year. By the 21st April 2008 edition of Raw, Senator John McCain had already been selected as the Republican candidate for November's presidential election, while Hillary Clinton and Barack Obama were in the midst of a battle for the Democratic nomination. The night started with something of a coup for WWE, as each of the three politicians addressed fans in brief video messages interspersed throughout the early part of the show. Admittedly all three videos are cringeworthy: Hillary told fans they could call her "Hill-Rod" and promised that if things got tough in Washington she would deliver a people's elbow, despite clearly having no idea what that meant; Obama asked the corrupt lobbyists in Washington if they could smell what Barack was cooking; and McCain threatened to introduce Osama Bin Laden to the Undertaker. I swear I'm not making this up.

Despite all the dodgy puns, the three video messages showcased WWE as a respectable company promoting the democratic process in a fun, non-partisan way... which they subsequently ruined later in the night with a truly baffling in-ring segment. Once again it involved political impersonators, this time depicting Hillary (accompanied by husband Bill) and Obama battling in a "Presidential Primary Smackdown". It started with a referee checking Hillary for foreign objects while Bill joked at ringside that no man had touched her in years, before a brief match ensued. Hillary turned out to be quite a good worker, hitting a leg drop on Obama for a two-count before he hit back with a Rock Bottom. Mercifully at this point Umaga emerged from backstage and beat everyone up to end the segment while the live crowd looked disinterested. On commentary Jerry Lawler said he hoped the same thing wouldn't happen during the next day's presidential primary election in Pennsylvania, which seemed pretty unlikely.

These occasional forays into low-brow political slapstick must have been frustrating for anyone in WWE who was trying to establish the company as a model corporate citizen at election time, especially because their efforts in that direction had otherwise been pretty creditable in the previous few years. In the Bush v Gore election of 2000 the WWF launched its Smackdown Your Vote campaign, a deliberately non-partisan effort to convince as many viewers as possible that they should register to vote. Admittedly there may have been something of an ulterior motive involved: the Attitude Era was in full swing at the time and the company was fending off criticisms from politicians and a pressure group called the Parents' Television Council (PTC) about whether its content was suitable for children, so it didn't do any harm for them to remind both parties that millions of voters were wrestling fans who would not take kindly to any censorship or other sanctions. Nonetheless, the campaign garnered positive publicity at a time when it was much needed and allowed WWF wrestlers to hobnob with starstruck delegates at both party conventions that summer. The Rock even had a brief speaking slot at the Republican event which was well received. The success of the campaign was such that Vince McMahon declared on Raw the night before the election that millions of viewers had registered to vote and that the next president of the United States would therefore be chosen by

WWF fans. He may have been getting slightly over-excited but there was no doubt that the whole endeavour had been a positive experience for the company, and they repeated it in the next two presidential elections.

The decision through the years to mostly stay out of the political fray, and to be strictly non-partisan on the occasions that they have got involved, has clearly been a deliberate one for WWE. Obviously it makes business sense to stay neutral where possible on the basis that taking sides in heated national debates would potentially alienate half of the audience, but there may be another good reason for its caution. Although the company sometimes appears to crave recognition and attention from the mainstream media, the reality is that when pro wrestling has become part of the national conversation it has usually been for negative reasons. While there have been a few positive PR moments, like when Smackdown became one of the first public gatherings of any significant size in the days following 9/11, most coverage of the company through the years has been negative, especially after the Benoit tragedy in 2007. The relentless attacks on the company seemed like they might be a threat to its very existence, but the only thing that eventually came from an investigation by Congress was some damning criticism and more negative publicity, rather than any meaningful legal changes to how the industry is regulated.

Bearing in mind how badly burned WWE was by these various incidents, its strategy of trying to fly under the radar when any major political battles were being fought in the public eye has probably been a prudent one for most of its history; most of the company's political activity was instead behind the scenes where it frequently made financial donations to both parties and recruited professional lobbyists to try and influence any federal or state laws in the works that might affect its business. However, as the company approached the end of the Noughties it would face a period of public scrutiny that was even fiercer than after the Benoit catastrophe and would eventually cause Vince McMahon to break his own policy of avoiding political comment on his TV shows. The reason? His wife and company CEO Linda McMahon decided to run for office.

OPENING A CAN OF WORMS

By mid-2009 Linda had already dipped her toe in Connecticut politics, having been appointed to the state Board of Education by its Republican governor - a move that raised a few eyebrows given her lack of relevant experience for the role. It soon became clear that her ambitions went much higher, however, as in September she announced that she was running for the US Senate in the following year's election. This meant there were two battles ahead: first, she would have to fend off other Republican contenders to win the party primary in August 2010, before proceeding to the general election in November where she faced the daunting challenge of becoming the first non-Democrat to be elected as a senator for Connecticut since 1982.

Although Linda resigned from WWE at the beginning of the campaign, it did not take long for her political opponents to attack her record as its CEO. By October the Democrats were using three videos from the WWE archives to question her decency: a clip of Scott Steiner on Smackdown in 2002 insinuating that he might rape Stephanie McMahon, Edge and Lita's in-ring "Live Sex Celebration" after he won the WWE title in 2006, and the infamous Katie Vick angle in 2002 where Triple H appeared to have sex with the dead body of Kane's girlfriend as it lay in a casket. Before the campaign was over, numerous other WWE moments would also be used against Linda including heavy criticism of the mentally challenged Eugene character, footage of Vince making Trish Stratus get on all fours and bark like a dog, and the build-up to the 2003 "Girls Gone Wild" PPV that WWE helped to promote. All of these were deployed to portray Linda as someone unfit for a seat in the Senate, a narrative that gained traction in the national press.

The McMahons' various enemies within the wrestling industry also spoke up against her. In November 'Superstar' Billy Graham campaigned for Linda's main rival for the Republican nomination, characterising Linda as having made millions of dollars by exploiting wrestlers while selling sex and violence to the public. "*She may look like a school teacher,*" he said, "*[but] Linda McMahon's hands are as bloody as her husband's.*" In December several former WWE talents lined up to question Linda's suitability for office including Chyna, Bruno Sammartino, Larry Zbyszko and Marc Mero. Jesse Ventura also chimed in, calling it "a scam" that WWE still classified its wrestlers as independent contractors rather than employees, which allowed it to withhold health insurance and pension schemes from them. Another damaging quote emerged in a March 2010 article on Linda in the Washington Post, as former WWF superstar Ed Leslie (Brutus Beefcake) said of her: "*If politicians are cutthroats and backstabbers and are not true to their word, then she'll probably make a great politician.*"

Perhaps most damagingly, no fewer than three former WWE talents died during the campaign. First, Eddie 'Umaga' Fatu (the same Umaga who had beaten up the Obama and Hillary impersonators the previous year) died of a heart attack in November 2009 at the age of just 36; then in August 2010 both Lance Cade and Luna Vachon died of apparent drug overdoses, aged 29 and 48 respectively. Inevitably these tragedies brought renewed media attention to the large number of premature deaths among current and former WWE employees - a scandal that was not made better by Linda's occasionally tone-deaf response to questions on the subject. When asked about Cade she suggested that blaming WWE for his death was akin to blaming movie studios for the death of Heath Ledger. This drew a furious response from Chris Nowinski, a former tag partner of Cade's who subsequently became a medical expert on concussions in sport. Nowinski accused Linda of kicking dirt on Cade's grave with her comments, and claimed that the company regularly rewarded wrestlers who used steroids by giving them higher positions on the card. As if this furore was not bad enough for the company, the relatives of both Chris Benoit and Owen Hart also spoke up against them. Benoit's father Michael wrote an open letter in May 2010 imploring Connecticut voters not to vote for Linda, claiming that she and Vince regard their wrestlers as *"little more than circus animals to be ridden until their value expires."* Meanwhile Hart's widow Martha launched a lawsuit against the company around the continued use of Owen's image in their output, which once again drew attention to the legal battle after his death which the McMahons had eventually settled for $18 million.

All of this negative press coverage did surprisingly little to dent Linda's electoral prospects, as she spent millions of dollars of the family fortune on her campaign and comfortably won the Republican primary in August. But as the main election in November approached and the intensity of the attacks on WWE ratcheted up even more, it seems that Vince finally felt he could take no more. In late October, just weeks before election day, he appeared looking tired and stressed in a series of poorly-produced videos on WWE's website and social media, launching a campaign called "Stand Up For WWE" in which he asked fans to *"set the record straight"* about *"negative and inaccurate attacks on our company"* by posting more positive photos and stories about it online. The campaign, which continued with further videos featuring wrestlers and employees on WWE television over the next couple of weeks, was a stunning departure from the company's policy of staying silent about politics and seemed to even surprise Linda's political staff, who issued a denial that they had coordinated with WWE on the idea. If they had done, it may have been a violation of federal election laws.

Ultimately it isn't clear what Vince hoped to achieve with this hastily cobbled together operation, but soon afterwards it was irrelevant anyway: on 2nd November 2010 the Democrats' Richard Blumenthal comfortably defeated Linda McMahon to become Connecticut's newest US Senator, by a vote of 55% to 43%. Having spent close to $50 million on the effort to become elected, Linda's campaign was one of the most costly projects in which the McMahons had ever engaged, and there was a risk that worse was to come: the state of Connecticut, now firmly back under Democratic control, threatened to conduct an audit into WWE's classification of its wrestlers as independent contractors. That threat ultimately amounted to nothing, but the damage to WWE's reputation from the onslaught of negative headlines that year was much more difficult to measure. This didn't stop Linda from running again for the Senate in 2012, causing another flurry of similar headlines and finally another defeat to the Democrats by a similar margin to two years earlier. When all was said and done, Linda had spent around $94 million of her own money across the two failed campaigns, more than any candidate in US political history.

TROUBLE ON THE HORIZON

Where did all of this leave the company? Well, since 2012 WWE has seemingly been stricter than ever in its efforts to steer clear of politics. However, there have still been a few storylines that gave a nod to real-world events: for example, the Zeb Colter and Jack Swagger characters in 2013 were clearly inspired by the far-right, anti-immigrant Tea Party movement that had sprung up in protest against President Obama's policies. Then in 2019 Daniel Bryan's heel turn was built largely around him lecturing fans about their lack of concern for the environment - a gimmick that Bryan later said was nixed because management decided it had become "too political". The company has also been embroiled in a couple more controversies that grabbed mainstream attention, namely the furore around the Crown Jewel show in 2018 and the classification of pro wrestling as an "essential service" in Florida during this year's coronavirus lockdown. Both of these incidents provoked media fury, not least from comedian John Oliver on his popular HBO show 'Last Week Tonight', which has become one of the company's most outspoken critics in the past two years.

Both of these episodes undoubtedly inflicted more damage to WWE's public image, so why did Vince McMahon decide to ride out the criticism in both cases and carry on regardless? While it's impossible to ever know the inner workings of the boss's head, it stands to reason that one major consideration may have been money: in 2018 the company signed a ten-year deal reportedly worth $450 million to host pay-per-view events in Saudi Arabia twice per year and a five-year deal worth potentially over $1 billion with FOX to produce shows including Smackdown for their network in the US. In the Saudi case, if WWE had declined to continue with Crown Jewel it would have been reneging on its deal less than one year after signing it, which could have cost it hundreds of millions of dollars and its long-term relationship with a lucrative emerging market. In the case of being an "essential service" during the COVID lockdown, it is not entirely clear what might have happened if WWE was unable to produce new content for FOX and its other television partners over a sustained period of time - but according to some reports, there was sufficient concern within the company about contractual obligations that WWE was eager to return to producing new shows as soon as possible. Financial concerns aside, perhaps McMahon made a calculation that in an age of short attention spans the media would soon move on to other stories and WWE could comfortably weather both of these storms. If so then he was surely correct - the mainstream attention was short-lived and does not seem to have created any tangible negative consequences for the company in the long term. In short, the benefits of pressing ahead easily outweighed the short-lived backlash.

Away from the company, Linda McMahon's decision to run for office may now be paying political dividends despite her two defeats: she became a member of President Trump's cabinet after his surprise election victory in 2017, heading up the Small Business Administration until she left last year to chair America First Action, a political fundraising committee focused on his re-election in 2020. The McMahons had a family photo with Trump in the Oval Office in early 2017 including Vince, Shane, Stephanie, Triple H and all of their children - one fan on Twitter pointed out that over half of the people in the photo had been victims of a Stone Cold Stunner at one time or another, including the President of the United States. These are the times we live in.

Given the McMahons' close involvement with the current administration, can WWE manage to stay out of America's political battles in the years to come or will it be drawn into lashing out again like in the "Stand Up For WWE" campaign of 2010? This is an open question, but there is reason to worry that political neutrality might become increasingly difficult in the years ahead. Whatever one thinks about Donald Trump, there is no doubt that his instincts are to stir up tensions in the country rather than to play peacemaker, and this could mean ever more volatility across America if he is re-elected. What might happen, for example, if the racial tensions seen across the country this year become even more entrenched and the type of boycott conducted in August by NBA players extends to other stars of other sports, including WWE? Pressure is growing on corporations in all industries to take a position on these kinds of hot-button topics and WWE may find it difficult to sit on the sidelines in those circumstances, especially if Trump applies pressure on them to publicly defend him.

What if Joe Biden wins? On the face of it, this might seem to provide WWE with a quieter life and fewer potential conflicts of interest during the next four years, but it would also mean Linda losing her position of influence at the top table of national politics. Worse still, recent developments will have given the McMahons cause for concern about the Democrats moving into the White House: former presidential candidate Andrew Yang, now considered among the favourites to be appointed Labor Secretary in any Biden administration, recently gave an interview to wrestling journalist Chris Van Vliet in response to WWE's apparent clampdown on its talent using sites like Twitch and Cameo to make extra income. In response Yang, a longtime wrestling fan, vowed to use whatever power he has after November's election to address the status of WWE wrestlers as independent contractors, calling the situation "*absurd and ridiculous and wrong*", saying WWE had got away with the status quo for decades, and ominously claiming that "the bill is coming due". If that didn't set alarm bells ringing in Stamford, what on Earth would?

Regardless of this year's election result, the precedent has now been firmly set that bombastic celebrities can have success in running for the highest office in the land. There have already been rumours about Dwayne 'The Rock' Johnson considering a future run at the top job, and the likes of Hulk Hogan and Jesse Ventura have both hinted in the past that they might run. We live in an age of such unpredictability that anything is possible, and the confrontational style of current affairs in the US nowadays is such that numerous pundits have commented despairingly that American politics resembles professional wrestling more and more each day. Perhaps in the future that will turn out to be more accurate than anyone could have guessed. Either way, it seems clear 22 years after the election of Jesse Ventura that the election of a pro wrestler to high office was not an anomaly after all - instead it looks more likely to have been a harbinger of things to come.

SIX TIMES WWE FACED NEGATIVE HEADLINES

1994: Vince McMahon's steroid trial: After a Pennsylvania doctor was convicted of supplying steroids to WWF wrestlers, Vince McMahon stood trial for allegedly being an active participant in the supply chain - he was eventually cleared of the charges but the ordeal shone a harsh spotlight on the company, with multiple stories of steroid abuse and premature deaths giving the impression of an organisation with a sleazy underbelly.

1999: The death of Owen Hart: Wrestler Owen Hart tragically died during a live pay-per-view after a planned stunt entrance from the rafters of the arena went horribly wrong. Questions about the company's safety protocols and about the decision to continue the show after Hart's death dogged the WWF for some time afterwards, and a messy legal battle ensued with his widow Martha.

. . .

2005: The 7/7 bombings and Muhammad Hassan: The 7/7 tube bombings in London took place on the same day that a controversial angle aired on Smackdown featuring the Undertaker being assaulted by a wrestler named Muhammad Hassan and a group of masked men who clearly resembled Islamist terrorists. The footage, which had been filmed three days earlier, aired unedited in the US just hours after the attacks and drew the ire of media outlets including the New York Post, TV Guide and Variety.

2007: The Benoit tragedy: After WWE main eventer Chris Benoit killed his wife and child before committing suicide, the national media went into a frenzy of reporting on the company's alleged shortcomings that may have contributed to the tragedy. As in 1994 the focus was largely (and lazily) on steroid use among wrestlers, but it also started discussions about concussions, wrestlers' rights as independent contractors, and a renewed focus on the large number of premature deaths among current and former wrestlers.

2018: The Crown Jewel controversy: In October 2018 WWE went ahead with the Crown Jewel pay-per-view in Saudi Arabia just days after Washington Post journalist Jamal Khashoggi was assassinated at the country's embassy in Istanbul, apparently on the orders of Crown Prince Mohammad bin Salman - the same leader who had been instrumental in signing the nation's long-term deal with WWE. The reaction from the media was scathing and re-opened debates about the company's business practices.

2020: Live shows in lockdown

At the height of Florida's COVID-19 lockdown, the state's Republican governor reportedly intervened to help ensure professional wrestling was classified as an "essential service", allowing them to resume producing shows from the Performance Center in Orlando while most other businesses remained closed. The move led to claims that WWE was being given special treatment because of the McMahon family's influence within the Republican party.

STRENGTH IN NUMBERS

Issue 24, December 2020

Dave Bradshaw

In 2020, WWE rule changes about its talent's use of platforms like Twitch and Cameo reignited debates about whether wrestlers should formally band together to improve their rights and working conditions. But if unionising is the solution, why has it never happened before now? Dave Bradshaw investigates...

In case you haven't heard this often enough yet, we are living in unprecedented times. Aside from the heartbreaking number of deaths the coronavirus pandemic has inflicted, it has also wreaked havoc on millions of people's livelihoods and caused entire industries to fundamentally change how they do business. Professional wrestling is no exception, and in some ways WWE has led the way in adapting to the new reality: its experiments with cinematic matches outside of an arena setting have (sometimes) been well-received, the Thunderdome at the Amway Center has been a resounding success, and in October the company's continued charitable work was recognised when it was named by PR News as "Corporation of the Year" at its awards for Corporate Social Responsibility. However, its treatment of talent during 2020 has been less universally acclaimed, with frequent criticisms arising about the precautions taken to prevent the spread of COVID at its tapings, a perceived lack of frankness about positive tests among its roster, and particularly about the April decision to cut costs by releasing or furloughing dozens of wrestlers, officials and other employees in the middle of a global crisis, despite the likelihood that profits would remain steady for the foreseeable future.

Perhaps most significantly of all in terms of the negative attention it has drawn, it was reported in early September that WWE talent had been "reminded" that they could not independently monetise their likeness by live-streaming video on platforms like Twitch and selling personalised video messages using services such as Cameo. WWE released a statement saying it was essential for them to "establish partnerships with third parties on a companywide basis, rather than at the individual level, which as a result will provide more value for all involved." These restrictions of online activity came as news to many wrestlers who are active on the platforms, and seemed to cause anger and confusion among some. Former women's champion Paige - who has almost 150,000 followers on Twitch - promptly changed her username to "sarayaofficial", apparently believing that she could get around the new guidelines by using her real name Saraya, but even this seemed to be contentious as WWE claims to own the rights to performers' real names as well as their in-ring monikers.

The aggressive stance from Titan Towers seemed mean-spirited to many observers, and even prompted former US presidential candidate Andrew Yang to threaten Vince McMahon with greater scrutiny of his "corrupt labor practices" if the Democrats won the White House in this year's election. For a short while it seemed as though Yang's intervention might have caused WWE management to back down, but an e-mail to wrestlers from McMahon in early October reportedly mandated that control of all accounts on third party platforms be handed over to the company by the end of the month. The Wrestling Observer reported that while talent would be allowed to keep a percentage of revenue from any such platforms, the policy was now that any such revenue would count towards the downside guarantee in their contracts - i.e. the minimum amount that they are assured of making each year even if they are not widely used on television and/or do not sell much merchandise. Given that there have been no live audiences since March, many wrestlers beneath main event level may not reach their minimum salary through their share of house show gates and merchandise sales, meaning that the revenue they receive through Twitch will simply count towards a sum that they were guaranteed to receive anyway. In short, those wrestlers are believed to fear that the revenue they had been earning from platforms like Twitch and Cameo will now be kept by WWE. Despite the obvious upset this was likely to cause, most wrestlers complied without publicly complaining: AJ Styles, Mia Yim, Cesaro, Aleister Black and Zelina Vega were all among those who stopped streaming on 29th October. However, Paige had strong words for WWE in an emotional Twitch stream that night, pointing out that she broken her neck twice working for the company, saying that she was actively investigating how to unionise, and saying she had *"gotten to the point where I cannot deal with this company anymore."* At press time it was still to be seen whether she would subsequently acquiesce and stop using the platform.

LAWSUITS AND MONOPOLIES

In hindsight perhaps it was inevitable that there would eventually be a crackdown of this kind on revenue earned from third party platforms. The terms of almost all WWE talent contracts have long been notorious for the degree of control exerted by the company, which routinely claims ownership of wrestlers' likenesses and real names as well as insisting on the authority to approve or veto external commercial activities in which they might wish to engage. This is particularly controversial because WWE classifies its on-screen talent as independent contractors rather than employees, meaning that it does not have to provide them with benefits such as health insurance and pension schemes which are routinely offered to those classified as employees. It also removes the legal right for them to formally organise in a trade union in order to collectively negotiate with the company for better working conditions and less one-sided contracts. Yang and others have argued that WWE cannot legally have it both ways, saying that if wrestlers are independent contractors then they must be free to sell their services to whoever else they wish; if the company wants the level of control and exclusivity cited in its contracts, it must classify talent as employees, grant them the accompanying benefits, and pay the employer portion of Social Security tax on their wages. As you might imagine, this was contentious long before the controversies of the past couple of months, all of which begs the question: if Yang is right, why have wrestlers not successfully pushed back against the company long before now?

To answer that question you first need to understand a bit more about American labour laws (I'll try to make this more interesting than it sounds, I promise.) A hundred years ago employees in the US had very few rights at all, but that started to change in 1935 with the National Labor Relations Act, which guaranteed workers the right to form trade unions and go on strike if they felt they were getting a raw deal, although these laws were amended to restrict the power of unions a few years later. Another law in 1938 guaranteed a minimum wage for most employees, and more recently in 1993 a law was passed granting most employees the right to up to 12 weeks of unpaid leave for sickness, maternity leave and other personal issues (there are no laws at all requiring employers to provide paid leave). In practice, some states have chosen to provide greater protections than these nation-wide laws require, and many employers choose to provide far more attractive benefits than the legal minimum. Regardless, independent contractors are not protected by most of those laws, which is why some employers are so eager to classify parts of their workforce as contractors rather than employees. Through the years there have been several high-profile court cases brought by workers who felt that they should be classified as employees, with mixed results but the general trend over the past several decades has seen increasing numbers excluded from full employment benefits thanks to their status as independent contractors. This may partially explain why only about 11% of American workers are members of unions – the lowest in the industrialised world – and the US falls below United Nations standards on the rights of workers to unionise, having been one of only a few countries not to ratify international conventions on the subject.

In many ways professional wrestling has long been a text-book example of the powerlessness experienced by many American workers and, to be fair, the issues date back much further than WWE's time as the dominant player in the industry. The creation of the National Wrestling Alliance (NWA) in 1948 as a governing body was partly an attempt to make the industry a closed shop, whereby those inside the club would deter competitors by sending their top stars to any territory that was under threat and ensuring that newcomers were quickly driven out of business. One of the founding principles of the NWA was to "act as their own commission to police wrestling", ensuring that "any wrestler who does anything detrimental to wrestling" could be suspended by the territory for which they were working, and that suspension would be enforced by every other territory too. In other words, although the territory era might seem at first glance to have been a time when wrestlers had plenty of places to work and could go to whichever promotion treated them most fairly, the reality was that a small cartel had a monopoly on the industry and any NWA promoter had the power to blacklist a wrestler who displeased them or who worked a show for an outsider. Meanwhile even the most modest of protections for in-ring talent were sometimes voted down: at the sixth annual NWA forum in 1953 a proposal was made that three dollars be set aside per wrestler per show to help pay for health insurance and life insurance. It was struck down by member promotions in a landslide vote of 25 to 5. The NWA is often credited with doing a lot of good for the industry by ensuring a certain quality of show and providing a means for territories to be kept fresh by rotating talent around the country. Much of this may well be true, but it was very much a club designed to benefit promoters rather than wrestlers.

The NWA's power waned slightly in 1955 when it was investigated by the FBI for its monopolistic practices, but the organisation was able to settle the case by voluntarily amending its rules so that any stifling of competition or blacklisting of non-compliant wrestlers was no longer written into its bylaws. Nonetheless, a lot of the same kinds of activity allegedly continued unofficially for many years afterwards, and it was certainly true that the NWA remained the dominant power in American pro wrestling until the WWF's national expansion killed off the territory system in the 1980s. The 1990s saw genuine competition at the top of the industry between WWF and WCW but since the latter's demise in 2001, WWE has often been the only real choice for wrestlers seeking to make their fortune. This has given Vince McMahon a similar kind of power over wrestlers' pay and conditions to that enjoyed by the NWA decades earlier, and it seems fair to assume that many WWE wrestlers may therefore have thought twice before raising any concerns about their status as independent contractors.

A TOUGH NUT TO CRACK

Still, a few have tried. Shortly before Wrestlemania 2 in 1986, Jesse 'The Body' Ventura suggested to his peers that they deliver an ultimatum to McMahon, insisting that he allow them to unionise or else they would collectively boycott the show. Ventura was starting to pursue a movie career at the time and says he had learned that Hollywood actors received far more in the way of royalties from video tape sales and other merchandise than WWF wrestlers did, which he wanted to correct. However, he has also claimed that his efforts to rally the locker room weren't just about getting more money from Vince - at the time he and other wrestlers were each paying around $5000 per year for health insurance (a huge sum in those days) and he believed he could get a significantly better deal from insurance companies if they negotiated a group discount. McMahon quickly found out about the locker room speech and apparently reacted angrily but in any case Ventura was about to leave the company to appear in the Arnold Schwarzenegger film Predator, after which he gained all the benefits of a union by joining the Screen Actors Guild so did not pursue the matter with his fellow wrestlers any further. A few years later he successfully sued the WWF for unpaid royalties from his video tape appearances, which is why his commentary has been removed from many WWE home video releases in the years since.

Another legal challenge to WWE came in 2008, at a time when it was still trying to repair its public image after the negative coverage that followed the Benoit tragedy.

Wrestlers Scott 'Raven' Levy, Chris 'Kanyon' Klucsarits and Mike Sanders - all of whom had worked for the company a few years earlier - claimed that they were owed compensation for being wrongly classified as independent contractors. Attorneys for WWE quickly moved to have the case dismissed on the basis that any lawsuits of this kind must be filed within six years of the alleged offence, and these contracts had all been signed more than six years ago. The presiding judge agreed and dismissed the claim on that basis, meaning that the case never really got as far as discussing the rights and wrongs of how wrestlers are classified. Having said that, the written verdict also referenced the fact that the wrestlers had freely entered into a contract with the company on the basis of being independent contractors, suggesting that they might have had a difficult time persuading the judge of their case even if they had filed it within the six-year time limit. Undoubtedly this was a major victory for WWE and probably served as a deterrent for any other former talent who may have been considering similar action. Nonetheless, another lawsuit was filed in 2016: this time over 50 former in-ring competitors led by Road Warrior Animal sought damages, principally for alleged brain damage suffered by each of them through concussions while wrestling, although they also attempted to take the company to task for its refusal to grant employee benefits to its wrestlers. Once again this latter part of the claim was thrown out because it referred to contracts signed more than six years ago, while the portion of the case about head injuries was dismissed in 2018 on the grounds that it could not be proved that the wrestlers' work with WWE had been the main cause of injury in most cases, nor could the company have reasonably known about the risks posed by concussions given the medical knowledge at that time. The decisions were upheld on appeal in September 2020, coincidentally just days before Animal passed away (it is not believed that his death was related to brain injury).

None of this suggests much reason for optimism among those who would like to see wrestlers classed as employees - and remember, under American law it is only employees (rather than independent contractors) who are guaranteed the right to formally unionise. The history of labour laws and the industry dominance enjoyed by WWE are both major obstacles to progress in this area, but there are other factors at play too. For one thing, any movement for change would presumably require the support of the industry's most influential stars to build momentum but that support is far from guaranteed. A New York Times article in 2010 noted that "*wrestling culture is infused with a tough-minded individualism, and some are ambivalent about organising.*" Moreover, the best-paid stars have a clear incentive to support the status quo: Ventura has claimed that it was Hulk Hogan who reported his locker room speech to Vince in 1986, at a time when Hogan was reportedly making more than the rest of the locker room combined. More recently, when John Cena was quizzed on the subject by CNN in 2007 he responded that "*nobody is forcing them [wrestlers] to get into the ring*" and that he thought the question of unionisation "*won't ever be answered, because I don't think it'll ever be asked.*" There have been a few influential voices who have spoken in favour of a union, perhaps most notably Bret 'Hitman' Hart said in 2007 that "*I'm a big advocate for a union in wrestling... I think that any wrestler that says they don't need a union is just a sheep that doesn't have enough brains to know they do need a union.*" While this sort of support from a retired legend may be useful, it is surely not as much of a game-changer as if Hogan had supported Ventura in '86 at the height of Hulkamania, or if Cena had had a different answer for CNN at a time when he was easily the biggest name in WWE.

Another problem is the unique nature of professional

wrestling, which is often seen by outsiders as neither a "legitimate" sport nor as a form of entertainment on a par with television shows or movies. From the perspective of a wrestler's bargaining power this is an important point: wrestling is not like professional sport where there is genuine competition among teams for the best athletes and where success is largely determined by their on-field performance rather than by decisions made behind the scenes (granted, there are some important exceptions – just ask former NFL quarterback Colin Kaepernick what taking a knee in support of Black Lives Matter did for his career prospects). The "big four" sports leagues in the US all have powerful unions too, making the power dynamic between players and owners very different to pro wrestling. The McMahons have openly emphasised the differences between these sports and their own product, having admitted as long ago as the 1980s that wrestling was scripted entertainment rather than competitive sport, allowing WWE to avoid some of the oversight and licensing fees imposed by athletic commissions in many states. Unfortunately for wrestlers this acknowledgement has not resulted in them becoming eligible to join Ventura in the Screen Actors Guild (SAG) because membership is only possible for performers who have worked on a TV show or movie that is covered by an affiliated union. This creates a catch-22 for most wrestlers: they can only join the union if they already work in a unionised workplace, which WWE certainly is not.

TIMES MAY BE CHANGING

So is it all doom and gloom for the prospects of wrestlers being able to unionise and/or challenge their status as independent contractors? Not entirely. It is possible that the SAG may follow the lead of UK performers' union Equity, which now allows wrestlers to become members and has taken an active interest in the industry, working with several UK independent promotions to agree codes of conduct relating to wrestlers' rights in the workplace. This is a huge step forward, although the weaker labour laws in the US may yet make it difficult for SAG to follow suit. Meanwhile, Andrew Yang's vow to challenge WWE on the subject is certainly significant if the Democrats win power in the election (which was still unknown at press time for this article), and more broadly a Joe Biden victory would probably improve the prospects of something approaching universal healthcare for US citizens - something that would be helpful to any wrestler who is currently uninsured. All of that being said, it is worth remembering that politicians have promised in the past to investigate WWE: during Linda McMahon's 2010 Senate election campaign her opponents in Connecticut's Democratic Party promised to investigate WWE's business practices, only for the probe to fizzle out in 2011 after she had been defeated at the ballot box.

Regardless, Yang's possible involvement is not the only reason for those seeking change to be optimistic: the formation of All Elite Wrestling last year is already showing signs of upending the industry, not least because it means wrestlers have an alternative destination if they decide WWE's contract terms are too one-sided. It is still early days for AEW but already it is clear that Tony Khan's approach to managing talent is different to Vince McMahon's: some of AEW's wrestlers are full employees with all of the associated benefits, while those who are classified as independent contractors are generally permitted to work elsewhere. Chris Jericho recently explained on his podcast that one major difference between the two companies is that AEW pays for its talent's travel expenses including fuel and hotel costs, which is something he says he never experienced in WWE.

And yes, you guessed it: AEW talent have been allowed to make money from Twitch and Cameo on the side without interference.

This is not to suggest that the issue is as binary as AEW being "good" and WWE being "bad" when it comes to looking after its wrestlers. WWE matches AEW in routinely paying for its talent's medical bills, especially if those bills are for injuries that happened in the ring, and there is no doubt that some wrestlers have achieved riches beyond their wildest dreams by working for Vince McMahon. Meanwhile, for all of its progressive early steps AEW management has thus far been ambivalent about the plausibility of full unionisation for its talent, and the company has faced criticism in some quarters recently for its safety protocols after two high-profile matches continued despite potentially dangerous injuries suffered by participants mid-contest. Those issues notwithstanding, there are signs that the debate about wrestlers' welfare has been rejuvenated both by the renewed political attention on the industry and by the existence of a new competitor to WWE which seems to have its talent's well-being at the heart of its mission. Will this result in real systemic change within the pro wrestling industry or simply be another false dawn? That remains to be seen...

EMPLOYEE OR INDEPENDENT CONTRACTOR? THREE IMPORTANT COURT CASES

National Labor Relations Board v Hearst Publications, Inc (1944): "Newsboys" who sold newspapers in Los Angeles claimed they had a right to form a union to negotiate pay and conditions. The newspaper owners argued the newsboys were independent contractors, and they were under no duty to negotiate with any union. The US

Supreme Court ruled in favour of the newsboys, saying they were indeed entitled to unionise. Congress reacted by explicitly amending the law so that independent contractors were exempt from the law.

United States v Silk (1947): The US government claimed that the Albert Silk Coal Co in Topeka, KS, owed employment taxes for the men it hired to unload coal. The company said they didn't owe any tax because the unloaders provided their own tools and worked only when they wished, so they should be treated as independent contractors, not employees. The Supreme Court sided with the government, holding that "economic reality" must be taken into account when deciding who is an employee. By contrast, in the same case, the court found that the company's truckers who owned their own trucks were indeed independent contractors.

FedEx Home Delivery v National Labor Relations Board (2009): Mail truck drivers claimed that FedEx should allow them to negotiate pay and conditions as a union. FedEx argued they were not entitled to collective bargaining because they were independent contractors who took on an "entrepreneurial opportunity". The court sided with FedEx, whose lawyer was future US Senator Ted Cruz. Interestingly, one of the three judges involved in the case dissented from the other two: Merrick Garland, who was later nominated to the Supreme Court by Barack Obama and was famously blocked by Cruz and other Republican senators.

HOW AMERICA'S "BIG FOUR" SPORTS ARE UNIONISED

Basketball: Founded in 1954, the National Basketball Players Association (NBPA) is the oldest of the four major sports unions. At the 1964 NBA All-Star Game, the league's first ever live TV broadcast, the NBPA players refused to take to the court until the league agreed to its demands about pension plans and game scheduling. The commissioner eventually agreed to their demands, and the live broadcast began 20 minutes later than planned! Disputes between the NBPA and the NBA over pay also caused part of the season to be cancelled in both 1998 and 2011.

American Football: The National Football League Players Association (NFLPA) was formed in 1956 and became the sport's preeminent union after the NFL merged with the AFL in 1970. Among its more famous exploits the NFLPA arranged a strike over pay during the 1982 season which ended up reducing the regular season that year from 16 games to nine. More recently the union represented three New Orleans Saints players who had been suspended for allegedly accepting financial bonuses if they injured opposition players. With the NFLPA's help the suspensions were eventually overturned.

Baseball: Several players' unions have come and go but the Major League Baseball Players Association (MLBPA) has been in place since 1966 and is split into three major divisions: a labour union, a business dealing with player licensing rights, and a charitable foundation. Working with the league it has developed policies on performance-enhancing drugs, which have been a major source of controversy in the sport. The MLBPA's most famous strike action came in 1994 and caused the World Series to be cancelled for the first time in 90 years.

Ice Hockey: The current National Hockey League Players Association has existed since 1967 (there was another union of the same name before it), and is perhaps best known for its dispute with team owners which caused the entire 2004-05 season to be cancelled - the first time in the history of US professional sports that this had happened. Similar disputes caused seasons to be shortened in 2004 and 2012.

PRIDE AND PREJUDICE

Issue 26, February 2021

Dave Bradshaw

As the wrestling world reflected on the death of Pat Patterson, Dave Bradshaw took a deeply personal look at the prospects for LGBT+ performers and fans in an industry that has a complicated past but a hopeful future...

I am gay. It might not seem like a big deal for someone to tell you that in 2021, but it's certainly a big deal for me: even now, almost thirteen years into an amazing career as a play-by-play commentator and journalist on the European independent wrestling scene, this is the first time I have let it be known in public and I still feel a little bit anxious writing it. While most (but not all) of my family and close friends have known for years and I have been fortunate to never face any negative reactions, it has still always felt a step too far to talk openly about it in the hypermasculine world in which I work. Indeed, when I did tell a few close confidants in the industry about a decade ago, most of them agreed that it made sense to be cautious about how widely I shared the information. All of them had my best interests at heart and shared the same fears for me that I had, some of which may be familiar to any wrestling fan who is a member of the LGBT+ community.

Principally I worried that people would think my only

interest in watching men wrestle was a sexual one. It seemed to me that straight fans watching wrestlers of the opposite sex are usually given the benefit of the doubt that their enjoyment is purely platonic, and that anyway there would be less stigma attached to any straight person whose fandom did seem to have a sexual edge. After all, if a straight man commented in passing that he was attracted to a female wrestler, others would not necessarily jump to the conclusion that his reasons for being a wrestling fan were in some way seedy or inappropriate. I doubted whether the same broad-mindedness would be so readily granted to gay fans. Additionally, as someone who works on shows and sometimes shares a locker room with male wrestlers, I worried that some might have a problem with me being there if they knew my sexuality. I was concerned that if influential colleagues were uncomfortable - however unfounded and prejudiced their concerns were - that it might affect my reputation and stop me from getting bookings. To some degree, I still harbour those fears while writing this now.

Of course, the stakes in my case are pretty low: I am not a well-known name outside of the relatively small corner of the industry in which I operate, and as a commentator rather than a wrestler I don't have the added anxiety of whether my opponents will be uncomfortable about the physicality of working with me inside a ring. I am also fortunate that attitudes across society towards LGBT+ people have been shifting at an accelerating pace for the past several years - changes that have undoubtedly been reflected in the wrestling business. Don't get me wrong: my own situation has been more than enough to cause me plenty of angst through the years and even now it is scary to be open about it. But my own journey to this point would never have felt possible if the trail had not been blazed by people much higher than me in this industry who therefore had much more to lose.

Both in the "major leagues" and on the independent

scene, the past few years have seen an encouraging number of people who have found the courage – long before I did – to tell their truth. Pat Patterson was one of a minority who found that courage even earlier, if not in public then at least among his peers, and found that he was mostly accepted for who he was. Yet heel wrestlers have routinely tried to draw heat from audiences through the years by behaving in an effeminate way, and homophobic slurs have until quite recently been commonplace among live crowds. This is surely one of the great paradoxes of wrestling's history – that behind the scenes the industry has (at least sometimes) shown a tolerance and inclusivity that was way ahead of its time, while its track record of presenting positive LGBT+ characters and storylines on-screen has been mostly awful, even into the 21st Century. Why has that been the case, and is it still true today?

A quick disclaimer before we start trying to answer that question: here we will focus mostly (although not exclusively) on how gay male characters and performers have been treated. That is absolutely not because the experiences of anyone else in the LGBT+ community are less valid but because, for example, the history of lesbian representation in wrestling is an important story in its own right, and one that deserves an author who is better placed to tell it. Even by narrowing the focus like this, there is still an enormous amount that could be said and no article could hope to cover every significant gimmick or angle. That being said, let's jump in...

DON'T SAY THE G-WORD

On 11th November 1947 the American industry changed forever with the national TV debut of 'Gorgeous' George

Wagner. Although straight in real life, the 'Toast of the Coast' decided to draw the ire of audiences by presenting himself as an effete narcissist. His hair bleached blond and grown out into curls, he would strut to the ring wearing sequin-covered robes as classical music echoed around the auditorium, followed by a manservant who would spray perfume around the ring to sanitise it for his master. He even handed out hairpins to women in the crowd if they swore allegiance to him. It was all a not-so-subtle attempt to play into the insecurities of the time: his femininity, pompousness and sophistication were the antithesis of what counted for "macho" in the mid-20th Century, and yet he won many of his matches and gained female admirers. It was an insecure straight man's worst nightmare: a "sissy" who could beat you up and might be more appealing to your girlfriend than you are.

This was at a time when there really was no such thing as babyfaces and heels in the way that is so familiar today - almost all of Wagner's notable contemporaries had clean-cut personas that were heavy on muscles but light on personality. By making such a radical break from that tradition and deliberately trying to antagonise crowds, it is not much of an exaggeration to say that he was the man who pioneered the entertainment part of sports-entertainment. Of course, he did it by perpetuating stereotypes and inciting deeply held prejudices for a reaction. In wrestling parlance, the "heat" was generated through pure homophobia - but it worked, and it made Gorgeous George a household name.

Wagner's success ensured that generations of heels incorporated parts of his act into their own personas: think of the robes worn by Ric Flair, the mirror-loving arrogance of an early Shawn Michaels, the perfume sprayed by Rick 'The Model' Martel, or any of a thousand other examples. That is not to say that all of these men were presented as lacking toughness - indeed, the notion that a preening egomaniac like Flair could be a prolific womaniser and an accomplished wrestler despite not being a rugged "man's man" provided yet another reason for fans to jeer. Nonetheless, in some cases the insinuation about a character's sexuality was clear, and the trend was spreading beyond the US scene: a lipstick-wearing Welshman called Adrian Street became a major star in British wrestling during the 1960s and '70s and is believed to have influenced David Bowie's Ziggy Stardust character as well as a host of glam rockers. Meanwhile, Mexico had its own tradition of androgynous characters which started at around the same time as Gorgeous George: 'exóticos' still appear in lucha libre to this day and are known for flirting with the referees, blowing kisses to the crowd and making sexual advances towards their opponents. In contrast to the portrayal of such characters elsewhere, exóticos are often presented as fan favourites, although their sexuality is still intended as a source of comedy and ridicule.

Interestingly, it was rare in all of these cases for any character's sexuality to be explicitly stated by announcers, with most promotions choosing euphemisms that offered a wink and a nod to the audience: Gorgeous George was "flamboyant", Adrian Street was "exotic", Adrian Adonis was "adorable" - but you would be hard-pressed to find anyone labelled straight-forwardly as "gay". They didn't need to be: it was an unspoken understanding between wrestling promotions and their audiences that anyone who seemed feminine must be gay, and that no-one who was a "real man" could ever be attracted to men. In this regard, wrestling was perhaps no better or worse than most mainstream entertainment in the 20th Century, which tended to present gay characters exclusively as camp, over-the-top and obsessed with lewdness. Speaking from personal experience, this could be one of the most confusing and damaging wounds inflicted on adolescents trying to figure out their sexuality - no doubt an untold number of young people struggled to figure out their place in the world as someone who was not attracted to the opposite sex but did not fit the mold of how a gay person was meant to feel or behave. For many it will have been a tortuous process. It certainly was for me.

Still, if LGBT+ fans had hoped that promotions would be less reluctant to admit the gayness of their stereotyped characters then by the end of the century perhaps they should have been careful what they wished for. The arrival of Goldust in the WWF in 1995 seemed at first to be just another variation on the same theme: his look was clearly inspired by drag queens, his promos were laced with innuendo, and he was constantly booked to behave in a way that was presented as deviant and predatory. On one occasion he gave an unconscious Ahmed Johnson mouth-to-mouth while Vince McMahon on commentary screamed that it was *the most revolting thing I've ever seen in my life!*" Another time, as they built to their match at Wrestlemania XII, Roddy Piper started an in-ring promo by asking his golden rival *"What exactly is your major malfunction, you fruitcake?"* and ended the same segment by promising *"I'm gonna make a man out of you!"*

At first the presentation was par for the course: Goldust was frequently described as "bizarre" and commentators wondered aloud if his act was really all about playing "mind games" rather than - heaven forbid - actual same-sex attraction. But then something changed: by the end of 1996 Goldust was on the road to a babyface turn and, with the WWF on the cusp of the Attitude Era, a decision was clearly made to address the question of the character's sexuality head-on. In an incredibly uncomfortable in-ring confrontation Jerry 'The King' Lawler outright asked him why he cared about another wrestler pursuing his "director" Marlena and asked if he was, *"y'know... well... queer?"* Goldust answered emphatically *"No"* and knocked Lawler to the ground. It seemed as though Goldust was only able to turn into a fan favourite if he performed a kind of reverse coming-out: as a fully heterosexual hero defending his lady's honour, no-one need feel uncomfortable cheering for him. That didn't stop the inflammatory language from Lawler though: a few months later in an interview he claimed Goldust's father Dusty Rhodes didn't love him because he "*went around the ring kissing men like a flaming fag.*" At least fans were no longer being asked to use this as a reason to boo - but the language was still a new low.

FROM BAD TO WORSE

Unfortunately history would repeat itself a few years later. At the end of 2001 Billy Gunn, already famous for his 'Mr Ass' gimmick, began teaming with Chuck Palumbo and it quickly became apparent that the two men might be more than just tag partners. They started wearing matching headbands and tight-fitting red trunks; they helped each other with intimate-looking stretches in the locker room; they regularly admired each other's bodies and adopted sexually suggestive positions with each other while the crowd booed them during an in-ring posedown against Stacy Keibler and Torrie Wilson. They even recruited Rico, a wrestler promoted from developmental territory OVW, to portray a walking gay cliche as their "stylist." Most weeks they were used in lame efforts at humour based on their not-so-ambiguous feelings for each other - the same kind of nonsense that had been seen in a hundred other gay gimmicks that preceded it. But then suddenly, after a match on Smackdown one Thursday night, WWE upped the stakes: Chuck got down on one knee, pulled a ring from his trunks and asked Billy to become his "partner for life" in a commitment ceremony. Gunn said yes, a smattering of boos filled the arena, and so began one of the oddest weeks in the company's history.

Despite the way in which the team had been portrayed

for the previous nine months, the Gay & Lesbian Alliance Against Defamation (GLAAD) embraced the storyline as a landmark moment in television history and helped WWE to garner mainstream attention. Billy and Chuck were interviewed on NBC's Today Show, featured in TV Guide and Variety magazine, and described in a New York Times article as "accidental crusaders". No alarm bells seemed to ring about how the company presented its LGBT+ characters even when, during the same week, Raw promised viewers "Hot Lesbian Action" which turned out to be two young women stripping in-ring and kissing each other for the fans' entertainment until a heavyweight male tag team called 3 Minute Warning interfered and brutally beat them both up. In hindsight perhaps we should have all seen the twist coming when the commitment ceremony finally aired on 12th September 2002: first the Godfather interrupted with his "ho train" to try and help Billy and Chuck remember how great women are. That didn't stop the proceedings, but moments later as the union was about to be confirmed both men got cold feet, explaining it was a publicity stunt that had gone too far and saying "*We're not gay!*" The live crowd was shown cheering and celebrating this turn of events, which concluded with 3 Minute Warning showing up again to beat everyone up, because why not? GLAAD claimed WWE had lied to them, Billy and Chuck's team ended soon afterwards, and once again pro wrestling told its audience that it had no place for openly gay characters.

To be fair to WWE they were far from the only offenders - in fact the Billy and Chuck fiasco wasn't even the worst thing that happened in the industry that year. On 23rd February 2002 a new independent promotion called Ring of Honor held its inaugural event, and the very first "match" in company history remains the worst thing I have ever seen on a wrestling show. An overtly camp tag team called the Christopher Street Connection (named after the New York street that represents a worldwide symbol of gay pride) arrived, clad in feather boas. Commentators Eric Gargiulo and Steve Corino reacted with rage: Corino said that if they wanted to behave in such a way they should do it in the parking lot so that no-one would have to see it, while Gargiulo said it was "disgusting" to see one of them kiss a male fan. Once in the ring the duo, named Buff E and Mace Mendoza, announced on the mic that no-one wants "our kind" in ROH (both commentators immediately agreed) before renaming the company "Ring of Homosexuals" and starting to make out with each other. The crowd started aggressively chanting the word "Faggots" and Gargiulo expressed regret that he was contractually unable to shout along with them. At that point a team called Da Hit Squad, a pair of heavyweights not dissimilar to 3 Minute Warning, hit the ring and decimated the pair before putting their valet Allison Danger through a table while the commentators bet that she now wished she had managed a straight team instead. The footage has wisely been edited out of the show on the company's on-demand service, as has a similar segment on a subsequent show, but 19 years later it should still shame everyone involved - it was so viciously homophobic that it is upsetting to imagine how much untold psychological damage it might have caused to LGBT+ people, or how much violence it might have incited.

Of course, fans were not the only ones who could be affected - the impact of working in an industry with a track record like this could undoubtedly take a toll on anyone. Chris Kanyon's case is particularly harrowing: debuting in 1992, he was gay but remained closeted to all but his closest friends throughout most of his career. Eventually becoming a regular in WCW, he went to great pains to keep his sexuality hidden, and on one occasion when a sexual partner recognised him from television, he even threatened violence if the guy went public. Other wrestlers noticed Kanyon's lack of interest in women and occasionally asked him if he was gay but he always denied it. That did not stop rumours circulating, and by the time he arrived in WWF in 2001 word had apparently spread to Vince McMahon, who approached him with an idea for a new gimmick. According to Kanyon's autobiography, the boss asked him to *"accentuate the wrist a little"* while bending his wrist to demonstrate. *"You have a very... unique way of speaking. You need to be very over-the-top and flamboyant... you know what I'm saying?"* Kanyon felt McMahon was trying to humiliate him and was asking him to be something he wasn't, but agreed to give it a go. He explained that after a few weeks of working on the character with one of the company's writers it was clear the idea was not working and it was dropped.

Sadly that was not the end of it. While recovering from an injury in 2002 Kanyon began to develop a new character for himself that would be gay but macho, breaking with the normal stereotypes. In his book he claimed that he came out to three wrestlers in order to pitch the idea, but that two of them then spoke to WWE management without his consent and the idea received no enthusiasm. Instead, once he was ready to return something quite different was planned. On the 2003 Valentine's Day edition of Smackdown, Kanyon emerged from a literal closet that was set up in the ring as a "gift" from Big Show to the Undertaker. Dressed up like Boy George for reasons unknown, Kanyon had been instructed to sing one of the pop star's songs as he emerged until Taker beat him to a pulp with a steel chair - an attack that Kanyon claimed gave him a legit concussion. *"Afterward, I was convinced the whole set-up, including the beating, was deliberate,"* he wrote. *"I thought it was a message from McMahon: We don't want you - or your kind - here."* Although Kanyon agreed to do the gimmick he later claimed that he felt uncomfortable about it but feared he could be fired if he turned it down. Afterwards he even asked to continue with it (an effort to gain a measure of control over his situation, by his account) but it was scrapped anyway and his WWE career never recovered. Kanyon clearly felt that management lost interest once he seemed comfortable continuing with the gimmick: *"I'm convinced that I turned the tables on them. When I said I was comfortable with the idea, I wasn't fun to torment anymore, so they did not allow me to do it."*

Before describing what happened next it's important to say that Kanyon's account of these events is disputed. Later in life he was diagnosed with bipolar disorder and displayed a pattern of erratic behaviour in the years that followed. Several people familiar with the situation have claimed that his career stalled because of poor conduct and insufficient talent, rather than because of discrimination related to his sexuality. Whatever the truth, the tale is a tragic one: in September 2003 Kanyon attempted to commit suicide but thankfully survived. He was released from his WWE contract in early 2004 but after a brief retirement he returned to the independent scene where he declared on a show in February 2006 that *"Chris Kanyon is a homosexual."* His intention was to become the first high-profile wrestler to be openly gay while still an active performer but unfortunately the announcement was botched: after the match he obfuscated about whether he was coming out in real-life or whether it was just his *character* that was gay. Although he clarified matters with a press release a few days later, fans were left confused as to whether the whole thing was a work. Kanyon retired again in 2007 and released his autobiography during the final year of his life, explaining why he felt he was released from WWE for being gay and describing how he had struggled with his sexuality and with mental illness throughout his career. On 2nd April 2010 Chris 'Kanyon' Klucsarits committed suicide in his New York apartment. He was 40 years old.

FINDING ACCEPTANCE

Obviously the picture painted here so far is of an industry with a bleak history in terms of how it has presented LGBT+ characters and themes to its audiences and, at least in some cases, how that presentation has made performers within the industry feel about themselves. Fortunately though, Kanyon's account does not seem typical of how co-workers have historically behaved behind the scenes towards wrestlers who were either openly gay or presumed to be gay. On the contrary, a lot of such wrestlers' experiences seem to have been broadly positive: for many decades gay wrestlers have at worst been tolerated in locker rooms, and at best have been openly embraced. Perhaps the most famous example of such a positive story comes from the legendary Pat Patterson, whose death in December has prompted plenty of reflection on his remarkable life. While it is true that Patterson sometimes felt it prudent to be discreet about his sexuality, he also found acceptance among those who knew. People who helped him break into the business such as Mad Dog Vachon and Verne Gagne found their initial prejudices disappear as they got to know Patterson and his partner Louie. Long-time tag partner Ray Stevens accepted Patterson without question, as did both Vince McMahon Sr and Jr when he worked for them. Patterson has even described making subtle references to being gay in his promos to get a laugh from his colleagues. *"That's why I never had any issues while with WWE when my friend Gorilla Monsoon or others would poke fun at me while doing commentary,"* he explained in his autobiography. *"I was in on the laugh from the beginning."*

It wasn't always plain sailing. In the early 1990s while he was a senior executive for the WWF he was among three company employees accused of sexual harassment by a number of young male wrestlers and members of the ring crew. Patterson was never charged with any wrongdoing and was later cleared by a company investigation. While the truth may never be known with absolute certainty, most of those close to the situation clearly believe that he was unfairly assumed of being involved with the misdeeds of others. Patterson himself felt deeply wounded by the accusations and later wrote that "*the fact that I was gay certainly played a part in me being targeted like that.*" He briefly resigned from the company but soon returned and continued to work there for many years. In 2014 on Legends' House, a reality show produced for the new WWE Network, he acknowledged for the first time on camera that he was gay. Even though this did not come as a surprise to anyone it was still an emotional moment and helped to confirm a sea change in the industry's public acceptance of LGBT+ talent – a change that had been set in motion the previous year when, for the first time ever, a WWE wrestler on the active roster had come out as gay.

It was a moment that was as courageous as it was sudden. At the start of SummerSlam weekend in 2013, Darren Young (real name Fred Rosser) was stopped for an interview at Los Angeles airport by a TMZ reporter who asked him if he thought a gay wrestler could be successful in WWE. "*Absolutely, look at me!*" replied Young. "*I'm a WWE superstar and to be honest with you, I'll tell you right now, I'm gay and I'm happy!*" The apparently spontaneous revelation was warmly received by the key names in the company: Young said that he was immediately embraced by Stephanie McMahon and Triple H when the news broke, and that Vince McMahon spoke to him for 20 minutes, reassuring him that everything would be alright and that the company supported him. In interviews over the course of the weekend several top WWE stars also offered their support: Randy Orton described the news as "awesome" and added "*it's OK to be gay, it's no big deal*"; John Cena said he was proud of Young for making such a bold move, adding that his own oldest brother is gay and is openly accepted by his family; Big Show commended his courage and predicted he would find a lot of love and support from his colleagues and fans. Young was soon appearing on Good Morning America and the Ellen DeGeneres show, where once again the response was overwhelmingly positive.

It was a moment not entirely without precedent: years earlier Orlando Jordan openly described himself as bisexual on his Facebook page and had reportedly pitched a character to WWE management that would allow him to express that on-screen - a version of which he ended up doing in 2010 after he had moved to TNA. Still, Young's announcement was the first for an active roster member who identified as gay, and for LGBT+ followers of pro wrestling it felt like an immensely life-affirming few days. It also seemed to clear the path for the next generation of talent in the company to be more open about their sexuality: nowadays Shayna Baszler, Sonya Deville, Jake Atlas, Tegan Nox and Piper Niven are all openly LGBT+ while working for WWE. Meanwhile Finn Balor's WrestleMania 34 entrance, during which he was accompanied by members of New Orleans' LGBT+ community, was another sign of the company's present-day determination to send an inclusive message. The arrival of AEW over the past two years has broken barriers too: their signing of Nyla Rose in February 2019 was the first time an openly transgender wrestler had joined a major promotion, and her women's title win a year later made her the first transgender wrestler to win a major world title. The company has also prominently featured Sonny Kiss, a gender-fluid wrestler whose character is a still-too-rare case of an LGBT+ person portraying a character that is authentic to their true selves. Most recently, in November AEW signed tag team The Acclaimed - one of whom is Anthony Bowens, an openly gay young athlete who runs a popular YouTube channel with his boyfriend.

. . .

Other well-known companies also seem to have become more comfortable in recent years with presenting characters who are at least implied to be something other than straight: today's Ring of Honor has come a long way since that horror show of a beginning in 2002, having featured the androgynous Dalton Castle as a babyface for much of his run, including a six-month spell as world champion in 2018. Meanwhile the success in NJPW of Kota Ibushi and Kenny Omega - collectively the Golden Lovers - during the past decade felt groundbreaking, even though the nature of the duo's relationship was never explicitly stated. Of course, while both of these examples indicate important signs of progress they are still cases of (apparently) straight performers portraying characters who are not straight. It has often been in smaller, independent promotions where wrestlers who are LGBT+ in real life have felt most able to experiment with characters that reflect who they really are. In the US there are now multiple LGBT+ characters and even a couple of promotions that are dedicated to featuring performers from within the community: the most recent example was during GCW's rescheduled 'The Collective' weekend in October, where popular indy star Effy hosted his "Big Gay Brunch" - a celebration of the talent and diversity within the scene.

The UK scene has also been ahead of the curve on this issue, with multiple LGBT+ performers and characters in recent years. A new promotion named Pride Pro Wrestling has plans to debut at London's Pride festival in summer 2021 (COVID-permitting, of course) and will feature exclusively LGBT+ performers and crew. "*I couldn't imagine that kind of thing happening a few years ago,*" said Reese Ryan, a 22-year-old gay wrestler who is a brand ambassador for Pride Pro. "I'm so happy to be involved and on that roster. It will be an amazing feeling to be part of that." Ryan's own journey in the industry has been a complicated one: worried about being shunned by his peers, he nonetheless came out to those at his training school four years ago and experienced mostly positive reactions. Nonetheless, for a long time he maintained that his wrestling character was straight - a fact that he attributes to some latent resentment that he still harboured about his real-life sexuality. In early 2020 he changed that policy, openly pushing that his in-ring persona was gay too, and he says it turned out to be a small but important change: "*It's not that I go out and do anything different to what I did before, but [it's important] just knowing that I could in some way be a role model for someone who's not comfortable with themselves. I basically want to be the wrestler that I would have needed when I was coming out.*"

Ollie Burns, whose alter ego Priscilla 'Queen of the Ring' is also on the Pride Pro roster, has been on a journey spanning almost two decades in British wrestling. First starting to train in 2002 at the age of 12, he came out behind the scenes at the age of 17 and soon started adding more camp and outlandish elements to his character. The response was mixed from colleagues and audiences alike: a veteran wrestler tried to throw him out of a locker room on one occasion before a show, only to apologise in front of the roster after seeing him perform, while a crowd at one show in a working men's club was so hostile that Burns wondered if he might need to be escorted through the car park afterwards for his own safety. More often, though, the problems he experienced were more subtle - backstage "banter" that was usually mild enough that he feared being thought of as oversensitive if he complained about it. He embraced the acerbic drag queen persona of Priscilla as a way of dealing with that: "*It's my way of joining in with it when the guys are making jokes,*" he said. "*I've turned myself into a joke, except I'm taking that joke very seriously.*" That being said, if the character began as a form of emotional armour, over time Burns has become more comfortable in Priscilla's skin: "*Last year I got some sparkly boots and I got tits for the first time - oh boy am I proud of them! I invested a few hundred pounds to help me feel good, and now it's a bit of a party. I've started to really relax and enjoy the character.*"

This hints at an important point: even characters that play into stereotypes can sometimes be empowering, both to the performers portraying them and the fans watching them. For example, despite all of its flaws, the Goldust character was one that Burns did not see as entirely negative when he was growing up - in fact it helped to inspire him. "*To think that you could be this overpowering masculine character but also wear make-up and have these ridiculous feathers and a wig on, it blew my mind,*" he explains. "*It created a lifelong fascination with mixing wrestling and gender play.*" While he later found elements of the Goldust character to be frustrating, this admission shows that things are much more complicated than camp, flamboyant gay characters being bad and macho, "straight-acting" gay characters being good - why after all should all gay characters conform to the heterosexual norm of what a tough wrestler is supposed to be? The key here is variety: it's not that Gorgeous George, Goldust or even Chuck and Billy are problematic per se, but rather that they become problematic when their heelish, over-the-top caricatures are the *only* type of gay character that ever gets presented, so that viewers are conditioned to believe that all LGBT+ people deserve either laughter or derision.

At its heart, professional wrestling has always had a pretty conservative worldview: the heroes have always been the athletic heartthrobs wrapped in a flag and espousing traditional family values, while the heels have often been anything that seems like a threat to that ideal: the foreign menace wanting to destroy our way of life, the criminal trying to steal success from those who have earned it fair and square, or - in the case of LGBT+ characters - the effeminate deviant undermining the very idea of what it means to be a "real man". Just as the rest of society has realised over time that the world is much more complicated, the entertainment presented to the public by our industry has made reluctant, inconsistent moves in the same direction. Yes, this slow on-screen progress is particularly frustrating given that the same industry has often been unexpectedly accepting to LGBT+ performers behind the scenes, but it is progress nonetheless and its speed has been accelerating in the past few years. *"I can't stress enough how much the mindset of everyone has changed,"* says Ryan. *"I remember feeling vulnerable, but I don't feel anything like that now. If anything I feel celebrated. I wish I could go back and tell my younger self that it's all going to be alright."* That optimism does not seem misplaced: after a torrid history, it finally seems as though pro wrestling is headed in a direction where LGBT+ characters are going beyond stereotypes to reflect the huge range of shapes, sizes and personalities that really exist. The industry is becoming a place where in the very near future, no real-life performer or in-ring character will have any reason to fear negative consequences if they are bisexual or transgender, or if they utter those three words with which I began this article: "I am gay".

LGBT+ RIGHTS IN WRESTLING'S BIGGEST HOTSPOTS

Part of the problem for LGBT+ wrestlers and fans through the years has not just been that they risked negative judgements from their peers, but also being stigmatised or even criminalised by society at large. Some of the most archaic rules were revised more recently than you might think and, even now, some of pro wrestling's traditional hotbeds still have a way to go:

. . .

United States: In 2003 the Supreme Court ruled that same-sex sexual activity was permitted by the Constitution, prior to which it has been illegal in 14 states. Some of those states still have not revised their own laws accordingly, and police have been known to enforce local statutes banning such activity to this day, even though this is unconstitutional. Massachusetts became the first state to legalise same-sex marriage in 2004 followed by 34 other states, and the Supreme Court mandated that the remaining 15 do the same in 2015. LGBT+ people were not permitted to openly serve in the armed forces until 2010, and transgender people were only permitted in 2016. Surveys show that while public opinion is now largely supportive of LGBT+ rights, it varies widely by region and still trails much of Europe on average. Discrimination against transgender people remains particularly widespread.

United Kingdom: "Homosexual acts" have always been legal for women and were decriminalised for men in England and Wales in 1967, although with stricter conditions than for straight people until 2003. In Scotland and Northern Ireland decriminalisation only happened in the early 1980s. Civil partnerships were permitted nationwide in 2005 and were followed by full same-sex marriage in 2014 (although only in 2020 in Northern Ireland). That being said, most churches still refuse to conduct such ceremonies and are not legally required to do so. The Thatcher government introduced 'Section 28' in 1986, prohibiting schools from teaching "the acceptability of homosexuality as a pretended family relationship" to their students. This was repealed in 2003. Transgender people have been able to legally change their gender since 2005.

. . .

Mexico: Sexual conduct in private has been legal in Mexico for LGBT+ couples since 1871, although laws against public indecency or immorality have sometimes been used to prosecute people. Anti-LGBT+ violence has increasingly been an issue in recent decades, with the high number of unsolved cases blamed by some on a lack of police interest in pursuing justice. Transgender people in Mexico City have been legally allowed to change gender since 2004, but only 13 of the country's other 31 states have since followed suit. Over half of the states allow same-sex marriage, and a Supreme Court ruling in 2015 has ensured the remainder must recognise marriages performed elsewhere in the country. In 2003 Mexico became only the second country in Latin America to provide legal protections against discrimination for LGBT+ people, after Ecuador.

Japan: The culture and major religions of Japan have historically been somewhat tolerant of same-sex sexual activity, which was only illegal for eight years from 1872. That being said, the country's record is poor in other respects: marriage is still legally defined as being between a man and a woman, and same-sex marriages that happened in other countries are not legally recognised either. Gay couples also cannot adopt and have fewer rights than their straight counterparts. Discrimination on the basis of sexuality or gender identity is not included in the nation's civil rights laws, meaning there is little action that can be taken if - for example - someone is denied a job due to being gay. Transgender people have been able to legally change their gender since 2004, but to do so they must be sterilised and undergoing sex reassignment surgery. A survey in 2018 showed that 65% of LGBT+ people in Japan said they had not come out to anyone, either at work or at home.

THE SHOW MUST GO ON

Issue 33, September 2021

Dave Bradshaw

As the twentieth anniversary of 9/11 approached, Dave Bradshaw remembered how WWE helped lead America's recovery by hosting the country's first major public assembly after the attacks...

It just wasn't working. For years wrestling fans had fantasy-booked a feud pitting the WWF's top superstars against its rivals from WCW and ECW but by 10th September 2001, almost six months after Vince McMahon had bought out his rivals, the reality of this dream interpromotional rivalry was starting to feel a bit, well, underwhelming. Nothing that happened on that night's live Monday Night Raw from San Antonio had helped to fix that problem: 'Stone Cold' Steve Austin still seemed too popular to be the heel leader of the invading "Alliance"; Kurt Angle's role as a heroic leader of the WWF side still felt less natural than his heel run the year before; the absence of most top names from the old WCW was still making the whole storyline feel watered-down. Those were probably among the main issues weighing on the minds of most WWF talent that night as they made the two-hour drive to Houston and attempted to get some rest before the next day's Smackdown tapings.

Little did they know that within a few hours such concerns would seem almost laughably insignificant.

"I'm okay, I'm okay, I'm okay." Still half-asleep, ring announcer Lilian Garcia thought she might be dreaming as she tried to make sense of the panicked voice in her ear. A resident of New York City, Lilian knew that the friend on the other end of the phone was supposed to attend a meeting at the World Trade Center that morning - but clearly something was very, very wrong. As she scrambled to turn on the TV in her hotel room, her friend explained that he had been running late for the meeting, and as he approached the twin towers he saw a plane fly into one of them so he just started running. Now watching the footage herself, Garcia looked on in horror as she saw one of the towers collapse on live television and tried amidst the noise on the other end of the phone to tell her friend what was happening. The line went dead, and none of her attempts to call him back would connect.

An hour earlier WWF executive Bruce Prichard had been in his room at the Hilton next to Houston's Southwest Freeway and was preparing to head over to Vince McMahon's suite for their regular Tuesday breakfast meeting about that evening's taping. As he got ready he had NBC's Today show on in the background and noticed something unusual - being in a different timezone to New York, the programme normally aired in Houston with a one-hour delay but for some reason this morning they were carrying the live feed. After hearing something about a plane crash at the World Trade Center, Prichard walked along the corridor and into McMahon's unlocked suite where he broke one of the boss's ground rules for these morning meetings by switching on the TV. Vince soon emerged from his bedroom and together they stared at the live footage of smoke billowing from the north tower as others including Jim Ross and Paul Heyman also arrived. *"As we all sat together in silence, which, for this group, was highly unusual, we saw the second plane crash into the World Trade*

Center," Ross later recalled. "*My mind wanted me to think it was a replay of the first crash. It wasn't.*" Almost immediately everyone in the room including McMahon started phoning to check on their loved ones - the company's Stamford headquarters were only 40 miles outside of Manhattan and almost everyone had friends or family based in the area. As the news worsened with another plane hitting the Pentagon, a fourth being brought down in Pennsylvania, and both of the twin towers eventually collapsing, it soon became evident that this was a day of unprecedented horror.

A NERVOUS NATION

Amidst all of this a wrestling show was the last thing on anyone's mind, but Prichard realised that something had to be done about that evening's taping at the Compaq Center so he called his contacts at the venue who quickly made it clear that the decision was out of their hands anyway - the city had declared an emergency and there was no chance of the event going ahead that night. It was still 48 hours until Smackdown was due to air on TV network UPN so there was plenty of time to decide how those two hours would be filled, but more urgently WWF officials needed to ensure ticket-holders were informed that they should not attend, and also that all of the wrestlers and crew knew what was going on. Some, like Chris Jericho, had spent Monday night in San Antonio and were driving to Houston as the news broke. He drove straight to the arena only to find it completely deserted, then went to the hotel to join his colleagues, who would now have at least two additional nights in the hotel with nothing much to do except watch TV or drink at the bar. In reality it wasn't clear how long everyone would be stranded in Texas, as air travel across the United States was grounded indefinitely.

Luckily for the WWF they were well-connected in the city of Houston: one of the company's close longtime business partners was entrepreneur and local celebrity Jim McIngvale, known as "Mattress Mack" because he used to wear a mattress in TV ads for his Gallery Furniture store. According to Prichard, McIngvale was *"the pseudo-mayor of Houston... if you really wanted to get something done in Houston, Mattress Mack was your guy."* On the morning of 9/11 he offered his services to the company, stationing some of his employees at the Hilton to help with any errands that the WWF needed running and also using his contacts at City Hall to help keep McMahon and his team in the loop. In particular, McIngvale knew Mike Thornton, a retired Lieutenant Commander in the US Navy who won the Medal of Honor for his bravery during the Vietnam War. Thornton was close with the city's mayor Lee Brown and was able to keep abreast of the latest developments as Brown had meetings with the emergency services and the governor of Texas over the next couple of days. He could also act as a conduit between the WWF and the authorities, eventually becoming instrumental in helping to ensure that the taping could go ahead on Thursday night.

It is not totally clear when that decision to go ahead was made, but its boldness should not be underestimated. Anyone who did not live through the week of 9/11 in the United States perhaps cannot appreciate just how surreal the atmosphere was in the country: people were nervous to gather in public places in case more attacks were coming; many doubted that "normal" life would ever return and some even wondered if a nuclear war was imminent. The idea of inviting 12,000 people to a wrestling show just 48 hours after the attacks felt fraught with danger, not only because of the life-and-death fear that the event could become a target but also because of the reputational risk that it posed to the WWF: what if the media called them reckless for hosting a large public assembly so soon? What if fans simply didn't show up to the arena? Regardless, Vince McMahon reportedly believed that running the show presented an opportunity to send a message of defiance to the terrorists on behalf of Americans everywhere, and after telephone conversations with the mayor, the arena, UPN and others, a live broadcast on Thursday 13th September was given the green light. "*It was a huge decision for Vince*," remembered former wrestler and WWF road agent Michael Hayes. "*[There was] a lot of responsibility on that*." Jim Ross agreed, describing McMahon's clarity amidst the chaos as "*the most amazing display of leadership... that one could imagine*."

WWF wrestlers and crew were all informed that their participation in the show was optional, with management apparently sensitive to the fact that many of their New York-based team were still trying to locate loved ones. Lilian Garcia had by now managed to make contact with the friend who had called her that morning but was still waiting for confirmation about the whereabouts of several others. She wasn't the only one: wrestler Chris Kanyon had a brother who worked just a few blocks from the World Trade Center and cousins who were New York City police officers - it took him some time to confirm that they were safe and assisting with the rescue efforts at Ground Zero. Tazz's wife and child lived in New York, as did his parents, and he was worried about the possibility of further attacks in the city. Plenty of crew members had similar stories and one member of the writing team decided to rent a car and make the 1700-mile drive back to Connecticut, but almost everyone else stayed. "*I think we all had the same attitude,*" recalled Booker T. "*That was to go out and perform at the highest level we possibly could.*"

Once it was determined that the show would go ahead, thoughts turned to how the occasion could be made as special as possible. While no consideration was given to bringing in any special guests from elsewhere (flights were still grounded, after all), it did occur to WWF management that there was one Houston resident whose presence would make a bold statement: the father of the sitting US President and a former president himself, George H.W. Bush. Through the company's connections in city and state politics, Prichard asked whether Bush Sr. could make an appearance to show support for the first major public gathering since the attacks. He was told immediately and firmly that the former president was in a secure location and that there was no chance of him breaking cover to appear at a wrestling event. Undeterred by this setback, planning for the show continued to gather pace – including a suggestion for Lilian Garcia to have a starring role. McMahon approached her about performing the national anthem a cappella at the start of the broadcast, a daunting assignment in the circumstances. *"He asked me 'Would you please do the national anthem? I really need you in this moment,'"* Garcia later remembered. *"Of course he would never force me, if I said 'I literally cannot do this' I'm sure he would understand – but I also knew that I had to do it."* As someone from a military family who was born on an army base, Garcia saw the opportunity to perform the anthem as an honour, and she steeled herself for the task ahead.

By the time Thursday night rolled around it was obvious that WWF really was out on a limb in comparison to the plans of other major sports and entertainment programmes: the National Football League, NASCAR and Major League Baseball did not return until the following week, nor did the late night talk shows of David Letterman and Jay Leno, and the Emmy Awards scheduled for Sunday 16th September were postponed by seven weeks. All of this undoubtedly would have added to any doubts within the company about whether such a rapid return was the right thing to do, and any frayed nerves would not have been helped by the additional security measures that the wrestlers and crew had to endure upon arrival at the building: metal detectors, sniffer dogs and even a briefing from local authorities about what to do if the arena was bombed during the show. "*Security was astronomical*," remembered John 'Bradshaw' Layfield. "*It took forever for them to scan the building to make sure there were no bombs or anything they suspected that was out of the ordinary.*" One thing that was no longer a worry at this point was whether fans would show up. The event had already been sold out when it was scheduled for Tuesday, but since the company had announced the plans for a "celebration of America" on Thursday evening, demand for tickets had soared. Over 12,000 fans arrived at the Compaq Center, many waving flags and carrying patriotic signs. Whatever the rest of America thought about WWF's decision to go ahead with the show, there was no doubt that Houston's wrestling fans strongly approved.

As live pictures from inside the arena started broadcasting around the country, viewers were greeted by the sight of Vince McMahon standing alone in the ring, dressed unusually for him in a baggy short-sleeved shirt and khaki slacks. "*Tonight the spirit of America lives here in Houston, Texa*s," he began, and over the next four minutes he delivered a rallying cry that was quintessentially McMahonian: defiant, brash and brimming with patriotism. For some viewers it might have been jarring to see this very real subject addressed in the same tone and manner as WWF superstars regularly addressed their fictional rivals; for others a wrestling-style promo against the terrorists was exactly what the doctor ordered. The speech also seemed notably self-conscious about any criticism of the decision to proceed with the event so soon, justifying the broadcast as being aligned with the guidance from "*our nation's leaders [who] have encouraged us to return to living our lives the way we normally do.*" Mostly, though, it was a rousing call to arms that captured the mood of that moment in history for many who were watching. The emotion was palpable as the opening credits rolled, with an even more intense moment just seconds away.

UNITED THEY STOOD

As the live pictures returned, an army of wrestlers and crew were filing onto the stage and entrance ramp, led by a man whose normal self-assurance was noticeably absent, replaced by a look of nervousness, even bewilderment - this was not The Rock, it was Dwayne Johnson, and on this night he looked as shell-shocked and human as everyone else. Next to him stood McMahon, and behind them a parade of larger-than-life figures who looked very different to normal: tough guys like Ron 'Faarooq' Simmons and Matt 'Albert' Bloom had tears in their eyes; charismatic performers like Jericho and Jeff Hardy stood still and solemn. Looking back now, there is a particular sadness in seeing several people among that crowd who would themselves soon be taken before their time: Kanyon. Crash Holly. Test. The voice that was about to echo around the arena belonged to another icon who has since been lost to eternity: "*Ladies and gentlemen,*" bellowed the inimitable Howard Finkel. "*Please rise for the singing of our national anthem!*" Standing alone in the ring, dressed in the colours of the flag, Lilian Garcia took a deep breath and began the performance of her life. Her voice cracking with emotion, she nonetheless belted out one of the most stirring renditions of The Star Spangled Banner that you are likely to hear. Tears flowed, hairs stood on end, and applause roared through the arena for a moment that remains one of the most remarkable in wrestling history.

After a quick commercial break allowed everyone to compose themselves, the broadcast settled into the pattern that would persist for the rest of the two hours: short, story-line-free matches interspersed with pre-recorded backstage remarks from those on the roster who wished to offer their thoughts. It was not a format that was totally without precedent - the occasion felt reminiscent of another sad night two years earlier when Raw took place the night after Owen Hart's fatal accident - but of course that prior experience did nothing to make this occasion feel any more bearable. Inside the ring the Hardy Boyz, Rob Van Dam and Booker T were among those who gained victories, not that anyone cared who won or lost. The Rock, now looking comfortingly back to his normal self, provided a much-needed moment of levity during an in-ring segment where he berated and eventually beat up Shawn Stasiak. Ultimately though, it was the backstage monologues that packed a bigger emotional punch than the physical action: Jericho appealing for a kinder world; Ivory reassuring the nation's children that the world contains more good people than bad; Kurt Angle saying that the men and women of the emergency services were the true American heroes. The speeches were not without controversy, however. John 'Bradshaw' Layfield's desire to turn another country "*into a stinking parking lot*" was received with loud support by his fellow Texans in the arena but seemed overzealous to some viewers, even in this highly-charged moment - the apparent allusion to carpet-bombing another population seemed at odds with the concern he had shown moments earlier for the innocent civilians who had been murdered in his own land. Perhaps even more controversially, Stephanie McMahon's speech involved her describing the attacks on America as analogous to the "attacks" on her family during the infamous steroid trial a few years earlier - a comparison that was felt by some to be severely lacking in perspective.

Still, notwithstanding these qualms, the show felt increasingly like the right thing to do as it progressed - by the time Angle led the crowd in a "USA, USA" chant to close proceedings and an impassioned Jim Ross signed off from commentary by declaring that "*it's time to get back to living our lives as Americans*", any doubts about the wisdom of going ahead with the event had presumably melted away. It had passed without any security incidents and the company's detractors would be hard-pressed to criticise the patriotic scenes that were beamed across the country from Houston on that evening. On the contrary, the consensus seemed to be that the show had been a triumph for the company. That is not to say that the story was over for the talent or crew though - they were still stranded in Houston with no certainty about when or how they would get home. At this point a few more took matters into their own hands, including Jericho, Edge and Christian who piled into a rental car and drove 10 hours overnight to reach their homes in Tampa, Florida. One company employee reportedly decided that it would be more economical to actually buy a car in Houston rather than try to rent one, and then planned to sell it after completing the journey back to Connecticut. Those few cases aside, most sat tight in the hotel and waited for the company to make arrangements on their behalf - by Saturday chartered flights were permitted if booked through a commercial airline, and the WWF apparently had the first flight out of Houston once the green light had been given.

Once everyone had safely got home from Houston, the WWF attempted to get back to normal with Raw on Monday 17th September returning its focus to the ongoing storylines. The events of 9/11 nonetheless continued to have some consequences for the company's creative direction: most immediately, the planned finish to the main event of upcoming pay-per-view Unforgiven was changed, with Kurt Angle now booked to defeat Steve Austin for the WWF title and provide a feel-good moment for an emotionally drained audience. A few tweaks were also made to some of the company's show names - in particular, the phrase "Raw is War" was phased out on the basis that references to war on WWF television were a bad idea, and the December pay-per-view Armageddon was renamed as Vengeance for similar reasons. Those adjustments aside, the company did not immediately change any wrestler's gimmicks to reflect the atmosphere in the country but it was perhaps inevitable that eventually some heels would use events in the real world to draw the ire of fans. The Un-Americans, La Resistance and (most notoriously) Muhammad Hassan were all short-lived attempts to do this in the years that followed.

It was only a few months after 9/11 that the WWF was renamed as WWE, but one thing that didn't change was the company's unapologetic national pride. In a way this was nothing new - from Hulk Hogan to the Lex Express, top babyfaces in the company had long been cast as flag-waving patriots. What arguably changed after 9/11 was the intensity with which the company pursued that association - the annual Tribute to the Troops show began in 2003 at the height of the "War on Terror" that followed the attacks, and is perhaps the most significant tradition from that time to endure in WWE to this day. Meanwhile, almost a decade after the tragedy WWE was on-air as news broke that the mastermind of the attacks had been killed by a team of US Navy SEALs in Pakistan. Immediately after Extreme Rules 2011 finished broadcasting, the company's latest all-American leading man John Cena addressed the live audience with the news that *"we have caught and compromised to a permanent end Osama Bin Laden."* The crowd erupted and once again WWE found itself at the centre of a uniquely American moment. Now, another decade later, the company is preparing for one more occasion with links to that darkest of days: on 10th September 2021, WWE is set to run a show at Madison Square Garden for the first time since the onset of the COVID-19 pandemic. Given everything that has happened in the past 18 months this return to the company's spiritual home would always have been a moment of symbolic importance, but the idea of performing in the heart of Manhattan on the eve of the 20th anniversary of the attacks will have special resonance both for longtime company employees and current roster members - not least for Zelina Vega, whose father worked on the 103rd floor of the World Trade Center and died in the attack. As for fans who are old enough to remember, that upcoming September evening at MSG presents an opportunity to reflect on an extraordinary two hours of television 20 years ago when a wrestling company led the way in helping America get back to some semblance of normality in the aftermath of unspeakable tragedy. For all of the sorrow and despair in that awful week, many still see the Smackdown after 9/11 as WWE's finest hour.

SPEAKING FROM THE HEART: Who Said What On The Smackdown After 9/11

"Tonight the spirit of America lives here in Houston, Texas... Make no mistake about the message this public assembly is sending to terrorism tonight, and that message quite simply is that we will not live our lives in fear... For we are a proud people, proud of who we are, proud of our nation, and damn proud to be Americans. And we will fight. We will fight for our families, we will fight for our rights, and we will fight for our great nation. America's heart has been wounded but her spirit shines as a beacon of freedom that never has been nor ever will be extinguished." - Vince McMahon

"I actually contemplated whether this show was the right thing to do. And once I contemplated it I decided that as the WWF family we need to do our job tonight, and our job is to bring smiles to the faces of all your families. And if we can do that then we've done our jobs. This can't be forgotten, it shouldn't be forgotten, and never will be forgotten, but if we can do that then this show was the right thing to do." - Edge

"I can't fathom or comprehend the pain and the suffering and the anguish that the families and friends of the victims are going through; the workers working diligently 24 hours a day, sifting through the rubble and looking for any remnants of life. It's difficult to talk about this. I will say that I couldn't imagine what it must be like to be there. I couldn't imagine if my own family were there. I will offer my condolences and certainly say that everyone is in my heart and in my prayers and I just want to say to everyone out there, again to the families and friends of the victims and everyone involved, is to just stay strong. Stay strong." - The Rock

"To be quite honest I'd rather be in New York City going through the rubble and seeing what I could do to help right now. But since I'm not, maybe we can help in a different way. Maybe we can begin with ourselves and... become a more peaceful nation and a more peaceful race in the long run by being a little bit nicer to each other... Hug your loved one a little bit harder or give him or her an extra kiss, be a little bit nicer to a stranger on the street, be a little more kind, a little more gentle." - Chris Jericho

"I want to speak to the young Americans of our country, the children: I don't want you to be afraid and I don't want you to be judgmental. I just want the children to know that there are far, far more good people in this country, in this world, than there are bad. America is made up of people of all creeds and all religions and all different beliefs, and that's what makes our country so wonderful and so diverse and so free. As a country we are going to embrace this tragedy, we will embrace it and remember it. Its devastation and its cruelty is what will challenge all of us to become a stronger, more connected human race." - Ivory

"We're running this show tonight because we're going to show you [the terrorists] that you cannot break, you cannot even bend the fibre, the backbone of the United States of America. There's going to be some critics that wonder why we run this show. I want to make this perfectly clear: go to hell. We're doing the show because we love America... You guys who are out there, we're going to find your ass. We're going to make whatever country's hiding you into a stinking parking lot. God bless this country, God bless this great state I live in, and God rest the sorry son of a bitch that did this. We will find you." - John 'Bradshaw' Layfield

"You know, all my life I've always wanted to do something special, to be considered an American hero, and after winning the Olympic gold medal at the Olympics some people would consider me to be an American hero. But after watching this terrible tragedy, now I know who the true American heroes are: they're the police officers and the firemen and the doctors and nurses and the paramedics, and all the people that stretched out their arms to help the victims and their families. They're the true American heroes. They deserve a gold medal." - Kurt Angle

"A few years ago, some people tried to destroy my family. They attacked my father's reputation, they attacked my mother's reputation, and they attacked the World Wrestling Federation. They tried to rip us apart but all they did was make my family stronger, and that's exactly how America feels right now because on Tuesday America was attacked. But America is a united nation and together we stand strong. I am incredibly proud to be an American citizen and I will stand up for my rights and my freedom." - Stephanie McMahon

"I don't have anything philosophical to say or anything that's going to change the world... I've had this bad feeling come over me ever since this whole thing has happened and it doesn't seem like I can shake it, but as a person and I think as a country, we have to shake it. We have to mourn the losses of the people that we knew, but we have to get the gears rolling again and that's what we're here to do tonight. What happened this past Tuesday was the worst thing that I've ever seen in my life." - 'Stone Cold' Steve Austin

MIDDLE EAST MISADVENTURES

Issue 35, November 2021

Dave Bradshaw

WWE returns to Saudi Arabia in October for the next event in their decade-long deal with the Middle Eastern kingdom. Dave Bradshaw takes a look at the troubled first three years of their partnership...

At 1:15pm on 2nd October 2018, a Saudi Arabian journalist named Jamal Khashoggi walked into his country's consulate in Istanbul for a routine appointment - planning to marry his Turkish fiancée, he needed a document to confirm that he was divorced. In the year leading up to the appointment Khashoggi had been living in self-imposed exile in the United States where he was writing monthly columns for the Washington Post, many of which were critical of his homeland's new crown prince Mohammed bin Salman. That might have been a dangerous game to play if he had still been living in his native land, but on foreign soil he had no particular concerns for his safety.

He should have. He was never seen again.

After denying any knowledge of the missing dissident's whereabouts for over two weeks, Saudi authorities eventually admitted that he had been killed inside the building, claiming that he died during a struggle with officials and eventually sending eight men to jail. The Turkish government concluded, based in part on audio recordings that intelligence officers obtained of the killing, that Mr Khashoggi had been the victim of a premeditated murder by a 15-man "death squad" who cut his body into pieces and had it removed secretly from the premises, having removed CCTV cameras before his arrival. Later a United Nations report said that the attack had been ordered by the Saudi government, and US media reported that the CIA had "medium to high" confidence that the instruction came from Prince Mohammed himself - a charge that he has denied.

A pretty gruesome story for sure, but what does any of this have to do with professional wrestling? Well, as it happens, quite a lot: the incident took place less than six months after WWE had announced a lucrative multi-year deal to stage regular supershows in Saudi Arabia, and the controversy was reaching its peak just weeks before the company was due to host its second such event in the kingdom, entitled Crown Jewel. What would follow was a torrent of negative publicity, including US Senators from both parties urging WWE to reconsider and a brutal on-air critique of the company from British comedian John Oliver on his popular show 'Last Week Tonight'. Top stars John Cena, Daniel Bryan and Roman Reigns all reportedly refused to work the show (in Reigns' case this became a moot point because his leukaemia diagnosis in October would have kept him off the show anyway), and the timing of Saudi Arabia's admission that Khashoggi had indeed died in their consulate coincided with the day that tickets for the event were supposed to go on sale.

WWE's handling of the situation was hardly a masterclass in public relations either: they initially released a statement saying only that they were "monitoring the situation", before suddenly removing most references to Saudi Arabia and Crown Jewel from their website on 19th October, right around the time when the ticket sale was due to begin. Six days later a statement was released saying that the company would "uphold its contractual obligations" by proceeding with the event, but by now all on-air mentions of the event's location were absent from WWE television and live crowds seemed to be booing every mention of the words "Crown Jewel". Stephanie McMahon attempted to justify the choice to go ahead in an interview with Sky Sports, claiming that "*it was an incredibly tough decision, given that heinous act... but, at the end of the day, it is a business decision and, like a lot of other American companies, we decided that we're going to move forward with the event.*" The reputational damage for WWE - at least in the short term - felt as bad as anything it had experienced for over a decade, but in hindsight the trouble had been brewing for a while. Even before the Khashoggi controversy, the relationship announced earlier in 2018 had already got off to a rocky start.

REAL PROGRESS OR "SPORTSWASHING"?

The Saudi regime's track record on human rights has long been a problem for any western company that has chosen to work with them. Women in particular have been treated in ways that are abhorrent to more liberal societies: among other restrictions they were unable to vote until 2015, banned from driving until 2018 and required to have a male guardian who made important life decisions on their behalf until 2019, although some restrictions still exist today. LGBTQ+ rights are practically non-existent, with homosexuality punishable by death or public flogging. Amnesty International has reported that torture is still used by the state as a punishment, and that one of the punishments for robbery is to have a limb amputated. Government critics are often imprisoned, and public demonstrations have been banned since 2011.

By the time King Salman named his son Mohammed as the crown prince in 2017, making him the second most powerful person in the land, it was already apparent that the new heir to the throne was eager to rehabilitate Saudi Arabia's image. In 2016 he launched 'Saudi Vision 2030', an initiative to reduce the country's dependence on oil by expanding industries such as entertainment and tourism. Within months the first new cinemas in the country for 35 years were being built, the first public live music concert in a quarter of a century took place, and plans for a Six Flags theme park were announced. Add to this the gradual reforms that were implemented to relax some of the more stringent restrictions described above, especially in relation to women's rights, and there was a growing sense prior to the Khashoggi murder that Mohammed bin Salman was serious about modernising his country.

It was against this backdrop that the WWE deal was announced in March 2018: a ten-year agreement with the Saudi General Sports Authority (now the Ministry of Sports) that would be worth tens of millions of dollars each year to the McMahon empire. There had already been a loose working relationship between the two parties for a few years, with WWE holding its first house shows in Riyadh in 2014. More events followed in the two years that followed, but this new collaboration was on an altogether different scale, and it was immediately apparent that both sides meant business. For the first show under the new relationship, WWE would take over the 62,000-capacity King Abdullah Sports City near Jeddah for 'Greatest Royal Rumble', headlined by an unprecedented 50-man over-the-top-rope rumble match and supported by an undercard that on paper seemed to be Wrestlemania-worthy. John Cena and Triple H were booked for their first singles match against each other in years, The Undertaker was announced for a casket match against Rusev despite the two men having no storyline history, and a cage match between Brock Lesnar and Roman Reigns was one of seven championship matches advertised for the show. It all felt a bit like the kind of fantasy booking that kids might invent while playing with their action figures, but by suggesting in the event's name that it would be greater than any of the 32 Rumble matches that had been presented in the past, some longtime fans surely felt as though the company was disparaging an important part of its heritage in exchange for a payday.

The inevitable criticism around human rights soon followed the announcement, particularly once it became clear that no women would be allowed to wrestle at the event. In response WWE CEO Paul 'Triple H' Levesque insisted that the company could help to bring about cultural change, pointing to the fact that the company had presented the first-ever women's match in the Middle East during a house show in Abu Dhabi a few months earlier. *"You can't dictate to a country or a religion about how they handle things but, having said that, WWE is at the forefront of a women's evolution in the world,"* he said. *"What you can't do is affect change anywhere by staying away from it."* Meanwhile the company was having more than its share of unusual problems with the male roster for the event, some of which reportedly stemmed from requests made by Prince Mohammed himself. Veteran wrestling journalist Dave Meltzer reported afterwards that officials representing the Saudi leader had requested that Yokozuna and the Ultimate Warrior be included as entrants in the rumble despite the inconvenient fact that neither was still alive. There was also some confusion over Rusev's involvement: at one point he was replaced by Chris Jericho in the casket match (he later explained this was punishment for a tweet in which he jokingly requested that Taker "bury me softly"), before being mysteriously reinstated. By the time the WWE contingent arrived in Jeddah it was fair to say that the build-up to the show had not been entirely smooth.

The broadcast itself was a 5-hour marathon and the in-ring action was fine, although the 77-minute rumble match perhaps outstayed its welcome somewhat, but some of what happened between the matches gave the show a distinctly odd feel. After both the Saudi and US anthems played in the stadium to open the show, commentator Corey Graves told viewers it was a night to "*celebrate Saudi Arabia's progression for cultural diversity in the Vision 2030 plan*," and Michael Cole commented that "*we'll talk about that throughout the evening.*" He wasn't kidding: everyone from John Cena to the Hall-of-Famers on the "all-star panel" were at pains to emphasise throughout the night how wonderful the Saudis' hospitality had been, and at one stage a slick promotional video propagandised about the "dawning of a new age" and a "societal renaissance" for which it credited Prince Mohammed. There was even a segment that indulged in the time-honoured wrestling tradition of using national rivalries to draw a crowd reaction: four Saudi prospects who had been at the company's recent tryouts in the country (including future Raw superstar Mansoor) were being interviewed in the ring when they were interrupted by the Daivari brothers, who strutted to the ring waving an Iranian flag and told the crowd that they came from "*the strongest nation in the world.*" They were quickly beaten up and dispatched by the trainees, and that was that.

To some onlookers this might have all been a bit sycophantic but otherwise it seemed relatively harmless. For others it was a gratuitous example of "sportswashing" - a word coined by Amnesty International to describe the act of an authoritarian regime using sports to improve their image and "wash away" their human rights abuses. Saudi Arabia was far from the only country accused of manipulating public opinion in this way: the 2008 Olympics in China, the 2018 World Cup in Russia, and various countries' Formula One grand prix races have all had similar charges levelled at them in recent years. Even so, the Saudi efforts to utilise sports in this way seemed particularly determined: in addition to their work with WWE they had started hosting major boxing matches, held a PGA European tour golf event, and were holding talks with representatives from the top US leagues in baseball, basketball and soccer about bringing their brands to the kingdom. This was a major initiative, and WWE was among the most prominently willing participants.

MAKING MONEY AND MAKING HISTORY

A quick look at the financial side of the deal might help to explain why the company embraced its new partners so wholeheartedly: according to an analysis of WWE's quarterly reports by Brandon Thurston of Wrestlenomics, the Saudi government pays the company about $50 million for each event, meaning that they have earned about $250 million for the five shows that have happened so far. That is more than the combined ticket revenue from every Wrestlemania ever, and almost certainly more than AEW will make from their entire four-year TV deal with WarnerMedia. In short, the value of the Saudi partnership is simply astronomical for WWE, and company executives must have felt in 2018 that the benefits of the deal far outweighed any negative publicity they would receive. Perhaps that calculation changed somewhat after the murder at the Istanbul consulate, but ultimately Vince McMahon and his team stood firm and chose to ride out the criticism. Crown Jewel would go ahead as planned.

Well, not quite. The second major WWE event in Saudi Arabia was - like its predecessor - causing some other headaches too, albeit none of them as serious as the Khashoggi issue. In early October the event was moved from a 68,000-seat football stadium in Riyadh to the King Saud

University Stadium, which could only hold 25,000 (eventually the attendance was reportedly around 16,000). The same arguments about the absence of women wrestlers that had been raised at April's event were once again gaining some traction, not least because there had been further controversy around the subject immediately after Greatest Royal Rumble: the Saudi General Sports Authority issued an apology to viewers for "an indecent scene involving women" that aired during the broadcast - apparently a video package including women wrestlers in ring gear, during which state television briefly cut off the live feed to domestic viewers. This only served to bring more attention to the issue, and by October some fans were even asking if WWE Evolution - the company's first all-female pay-per-view which took place just a few days prior to the male roster flying to Riyadh - was being held as a direct response to criticisms about the Saudi project. The charge seemed harsh considering the increased focus that had been given to the women's division in the months and years leading to the event, but Triple H felt sufficiently stung by the criticism that he made a point of publicly making it clear that the timing of the two events was not related.

Meanwhile the return of two WWE legends at the show was causing quite a stir: Hulk Hogan, whose relationship with WWE had been terminated in 2015 after audio footage emerged of him uttering racial slurs, had recently been brought back into the fold and was announced as the host of Crown Jewel - a decision that was far from universally popular. But perhaps most notably, more than eight years after his memorable retirement match at Wrestlemania XXVI, Shawn Michaels had agreed to return to the ring for a tag match with Triple H against the Undertaker and Kane. The reactions to this news were mixed: plenty of fans were excited to see the Heartbreak Kid back inside a wrestling ring, but to others it seemed a shame to tarnish such a perfect end to his career by adding this unexpected footnote. Inevitably some pundits speculated that he had been persuaded to go ahead with the match by a massive payday, but Michaels later denied that this was his motivation, claiming on Edge and Christian's podcast that he saw the event as a one-off opportunity to deliver his "greatest hits" alongside other legends with whom he was very familiar. Unfortunately for everyone involved the match would turn out to be one of the most shambolic of any of their careers.

The crowd was fired up to see four icons in the main event of the show, especially after an unpopular end to the night's 8-man tournament moments earlier, in which Shane McMahon had been crowned the winner of WWE's 'World Cup'. The high-profile tag team showdown was booked to run for almost half an hour, but it wasn't long after the opening bell that things started to unravel: on a spill over the top rope to the floor Triple H tore his pectoral muscle and, despite his best efforts, was unable to do very much for the rest of the match. This left Michaels to carry the load in his first match for almost a decade, but even for one of the greatest of all time ring rust was a factor. Several spots were blown, and at one point while delivering some punches on the top turnbuckle, HBK grabbed a handful of Kane's wig and accidentally removed his attached mask. By the time DX scored the pinfall to end the night, all four men knew it had been a bad night at the office. "*It totally blew*," reflected Michaels later. "*It's like a bad comedy movie*," said Triple H of how it felt to watch the match back. Undertaker also concurred: "*It was a total train wreck*," he said. "*It was a disaster*." For an event that seemed to have been cursed from the moment it was announced, this somehow seemed like an appropriate ending.

Unfortunately for Undertaker, it wouldn't be the last time he featured in a poorly-received main event in Saudi Arabia. The next WWE show in the country was a return to Jeddah in June 2019 for 'Super ShowDown' and for the first time ever the Dead Man was set to face Goldberg, who had returned to the ring for a programme with Brock Lesnar in 2016 and was inducted into the Hall of Fame in 2018. Still, the match against 'Taker would be his first in over two years and, disastrously, it would be the second consecutive main event of a WWE Saudi show that was derailed by an early injury. This time the problem arose when Goldberg headbutted the steel ring post by accident, giving himself a head wound and concussion. This left him disoriented for the rest of the match, and the consequences were almost tragic – while performing his trademark jackhammer move, Goldberg came within centimetres of dropping Undertaker on his head in a nasty near-miss. There were several other botches too, and the end came after a choke slam for which Goldberg barely managed to leap into the air. Afterwards the former WCW champion called it "*a perfect storm of crappiness*".

Still, if the worst thing that happened at Super Show-Down was that its main event failed to deliver then presumably WWE must have considered the experience to be a considerable improvement on all the problems that plagued Crown Jewel the previous autumn. In fact, the company came close to a major PR victory at the show: Natalya and Alexa Bliss flew with the crew to Jeddah amidst high hopes that they would be permitted to stage the first ever women's match in Saudi Arabia, only for government officials to nix the plan prior to the big night. Fortunately the company would have more luck when they again pushed for a women's match upon their return to the kingdom for the fourth major event of their partnership on 31st October 2019. At a press conference on the eve of the show WWE announced that Natalya would face Lacey Evans in a historic contest the following night. Stephanie McMahon explained that both women would wear full bodysuits rather than their usual attire, out of respect for their hosts' culture. Nonetheless, she seemed genuinely delighted about the news. "*As a woman, as a mother, as just a person, I couldn't be more proud,*" she told TMZ. "I *am ecstatic, I am thrilled, I am many different adjectives to describe how I feel right now.*" The following night when the match took place it was warmly received by the live crowd (aside from one plastic bottle thrown at Natalya during her entrance) and really did have the feel of an important moment. It was also a vindication of sorts for WWE officials who had responded to previous criticism by promising that they were pushing for change with their Saudi partners. Eventually they got their way and produced a moment that is surely the high point of the company's work in the country so far.

TRAVEL TROUBLES

In fact, almost everything about Crown Jewel 2019 felt better than the previous year: this time it had not been moved to a smaller venue, taking place in the 68,000-capacity stadium where the 2018 show was originally supposed to happen. The critical reviews were much improved too, with particular praise reserved for hometown hero Mansoor's singles victory over Cesaro. Two high-profile celebrities from other combat sports also had matches on the broadcast: neither MMA star Cain Velasquez nor boxer Tyson Fury had particularly memorable in-ring debuts for WWE, but the presence of both men helped to provide some much-needed positive mainstream media coverage to complement the plaudits the company received for the women's match. At last it seemed as though the tide was turning for a partnership that had previously been blighted by one setback after another... but then came the journey home.

The details of what happened in the hours after the event ended are still contested, but they revolve around the fact that most of WWE's talent and staff suffered a lengthy delay in flying back to the US. The plan had been to return immediately after the pay-per-view so that everyone would be back in time for Smackdown in Buffalo, New York, the next evening. Unfortunately their flight was not cleared to take off and they spent the entire night either in the airport terminal or sitting in the plane on the runway, before being taken to a hotel to sleep for a few hours and finally taking off around a day later than planned. As the ordeal unfolded several WWE stars used social media to express their frustration, with some seeming to hint at annoyance about the fact that Vince McMahon and some of the company's biggest stars had left the country on private planes before the problems started.

A press release from the company blamed the delays on mechanical failures, and their version of events was backed up by the flight's operators Atlas Air, but soon rumours started flying about other reasons for the drama. Dave Meltzer reported that there had been a disagreement on the day of the show between Vince McMahon and the Saudi authorities about an alleged late payment for the company's previous show in the country. Then, Meltzer said, when the money had still not been received by show time McMahon had ordered the live feed of the show to be blocked to viewers in the country until the issue was resolved, causing the broadcast to eventually air on a 40-minute tape delay. The theory goes that Prince Mohammed bin Salman was so infuriated by this move that he would not allow the WWE plane to leave the country. An anonymous ex-WWE wrestler confirmed the reports in a statement as part of a lawsuit against the company in 2020 – an account that WWE dismissed as "phony" claims from a *disgruntled former wrestler with no knowledge of the facts.*" In August 2021, former WWE wrestler Tucker (real name Levi Cooper) also said that those media reports matched his general understanding of what happened on that night.

Whatever the truth, the delay caused almost all of the main roster to miss Smackdown and forced NXT wrestlers to be drafted into the show in their place at short notice. Despite this, the whole episode apparently did not do any long-term damage to the relationship between WWE and Saudi Arabia, which continued into 2020 with a second Super ShowDown at the end of February. This time there were no travel issues and the event passed largely without incident, the only real controversy after the event being about creative decisions in the two top championship matches: Goldberg defeated red-hot heel character 'The Fiend' for the Universal Championship and Brock Lesnar bulldozed through Ricochet in 90 seconds, both of which raised eyebrows among many fans. The event also featured another women's match, this time between Bailey and Naomi, and a surprise cameo by the Undertaker in the show-opening gauntlet match. Of course, shortly after that event the COVID pandemic brought a halt to all international travel, and the upcoming return to Riyadh for Crown Jewel 2021 on 21st October will be the first time WWE has made the journey to the Middle East for over a year and a half.

One big question headed into that event is whether the next few years of the partnership between WWE and Saudi Arabia will be as turbulent as these early years have been. There certainly are no signs that either side wishes to back out of the agreement – on the contrary, Vince McMahon announced on Twitter less than a week after the travel fiasco at Crown Jewel 2019 that the scope of the deal had been expanded, with two large-scale events now confirmed to take place in Saudi Arabia every year until at least 2027. Meanwhile Prince Mohammed is pressing ahead with his plans to boost his country's involvement in sports and entertainment: the first Saudi Arabian Grand Prix is scheduled for this December, he has invested over $3 billion in video games companies including Activision Blizzard and Electronic Arts, and in 2020 he even tried to buy Newcastle United Football Club. It is clear that WWE is just one part of a much larger vision for an increasingly outward-looking Saudi Arabian regime, but it is an important part and the alliance has provided no shortage of heated debate. With so much intrigue already generated by the early years of WWE's most lucrative live events deal in history, it seems destined to remain a fascinating and volatile story for many years to come.

THE TITUS SLIP-UP SEEN WORLDWIDE

Spare a thought for Titus O'Neil. Although more recently he has been recognised by WWE for his charity work with the Warrior Award at the Hall of Fame ceremony, back in 2018 his career was still recovering from a bizarre incident two years earlier when he was suspended for 60 days after grabbing Vince McMahon in an apparent attempt at some on-air humour during Daniel Bryan's retirement celebration on Raw. By the time of WWE's Greatest Royal Rumble he was back in the good graces but still in search of a moment that could define his in-ring career. One crazy moment on his way to the ring in Jeddah that night was about to change all that.

Entering at number 39, Titus charged down the ramp towards the ring at high speed but then somehow tripped up a few feet short of the ring, causing him to stumble forwards, fall on his front and slide almost fully under the apron. The commentary team lost the plot for several minutes and there followed a barrage of slow motion replays of the incident as almost everyone temporarily lost interest in the live action.

WWE still wasn't finished: Titus was booked to slip up again as he entered the ring on the next week's Raw, while the company's social media team helpfully released more video clips showing the embarrassing stumble from every conceivable angle. Cathy Kelley even hosted a video offering "in-depth analysis" of the moment including tweets from other WWE stars, and revealed that WWE Shop had produced a t-shirt to commemorate the occasion. Was this overkill? Not at all - it was the birth of a timeless internet meme, and as Michael Cole said at the time, it "may be the greatest moment in Royal Rumble history. It really might be the greatest moment ever."

DEALING WITH DIFFERENCE

Issue 47, February 2023

Adam Pearson & Dave Bradshaw

Professional wrestling has something of a chequered history when it comes to portraying characters who have disabilities or visible differences. Actor, presenter and campaigner Adam Pearson teamed up with WrestleTalk's Dave Bradshaw to take a look at some of the most notable moments in the industry's efforts, both good and bad...

Dating back to its origins on the carnival circuit, the pro wrestling business has always been fond of presenting 'special attractions' that will wow its audiences. For many years Andre the Giant was one of the most popular draws in the industry, with crowds flocking to witness a character who was quite literally larger-than-life because of his gigantism. At other times wrestling fans have paid to see those who are smaller, heavier, or otherwise different to the average person they encounter in everyday life - and more often than not promoters have been eager to sell tickets on the basis of that difference.

In response to this you might say: "So what? It's just entertainment" - and there is no doubt that many of those in wrestling who either have real-life disabilities or have portrayed characters with such traits have done so of their own free will, happy to make a living from the curiosity of paying customers. However, recent years have seen a growing trend towards understanding how the impact of these characters reaches far beyond the TV screen, with the potential to have a profound effect on the communities they represent. In some places those communities have taken matters into their own hands: a fascinating 2015 documentary by filmmaker Heath Cozens explored the world of Doglegs, an independent Japanese promotion in which people with various disabilities compete against able-bodied opponents in a hybrid of pro wrestling and MMA-style fighting. Responses to the people featured in the documentary were mixed: were those involved in Doglegs being exploited, or were they smashing stereotypes?

In Doglegs' case you can decide for yourself (the movie is available at doglegsmovie.com), but regardless of your view the debate around that film is emblematic of a wider discussion about the appropriate way to represent disabled people within wrestling. Can the industry be a force for good in how it presents difference, and how has it fared in the past? Let's take a look...

A LITTLE RESPECT

One of the most popular wrestling attractions in the middle of the 20th Century - and one of the more controversial ones in the 21st Century - has been the use of little people in pro wrestling shows. Even the name used for this is contentious: it has historically been described as 'midget wrestling' but the term 'midget' is considered offensive by many in the dwarfism community. Still, a few promotions still use the word to this day - and some little wrestlers are comfortable with it, saying that the term draws in more fans than calling it 'little people wrestling'. Indeed, Dylan Postl - better known to WWE fans as Hornswoggle - put it simply in an interview with Sports Illustrated in 2017: "*The word midget makes me money*."

Whatever term you choose to use today, the attraction then known as midget wrestling had its heyday in the 1950s and 1960s, at least on the North American scene, with at least two groups of little people passing between NWA territories as a touring attraction. In fact, the NWA even had a 'World Midget's Championship' from 1949 which stayed active for 50 years. Little wrestlers were such a draw that promoters were willing to pay large sums for their services: for example, in-ring rivals Sky Low Low and Little Beaver routinely demanded 15% of a show's ticket revenue at the peak of their popularity. According to wrestling lore, that duo once even wrestled in front of Queen Elizabeth II and King Farouk of Egypt - although it's possible that this is an urban legend, as little information about the match seems to exist. Both men were later inducted into the Professional Wrestling Hall of Fame (a separate entity to the WWE Hall of Fame), as were fellow little wrestlers Lord Littlebrook and Fuzzy Cupid.

This type of wrestling remained relatively popular in the 1980s, including at Wrestlemania III when Little Beaver was famously slammed by the much larger King Kong Bundy, and even in the 1990s when Doink the Clown was joined by a mini-version of his own character called Dink. WWE (then WWF) also had a deal with Mexican promotion AAA in the late 90s which saw some of the little wrestlers from the latter's roster featured on American TV, including in matches at the Royal Rumble in both 1997 and 1998. After that their use declined in the US, although not in Mexico where both AAA and rival promotion CMLL continue to feature little wrestlers and both have a World 'Mini-Estrella' Championship. In CMLL's case that title has existed for 30 years.

One of the main criticisms of little people wrestling has been that throughout history and across most promotions where they have been featured, they have commonly been treated as comic relief, competing in matches filled with slapstick physical humour such as running between the referee's legs, biting an opponent's rear end or dogpiling on top of each other to pin a larger opponent. Campaigners have said this reinforces the stereotype that little people are worthy of ridicule from others. By advertising little wrestlers on the basis of their size rather than their ability, promoters arguably reinforce a habit that dates back to wrestling's roots in carnivals where members of the public paid to stare at 'oddities' who were physically different to others in one way or another.

Even WWE's later efforts to feature a 'juniors division' did little to rebut that criticism. In a backstage skit during an episode of Smackdown in October 2005, a 'network executive' named Palmer Canon told general manager Teddy Long that he was introducing a new division, at which point four little wrestlers charged into the room and started jumping up and down on the nearby sofa. One of them, Super Porky, was tucking into a giant ham - and all of them were treated as little more than comic relief. Over the next few weeks Smackdown sporadically featured a juniors' division match, complete with questionable lines on commentary such as Tazz asking Canon: "*Is there a little island somewhere where you keep these guys, like in a cage or something?*" By February the company seemed to have judged that the joke had worn thin, and the idea was quietly dropped.

Three months after that came the debut of perhaps WWE's best-known little person. Initially called 'Little Bastard', Dylan Postl was initially presented as a feral leprechaun who lived under the ring and was a sidekick to Irish wrestler Finlay. By early 2007 he was renamed as Hornswoggle, and went on to be a part of several memorable storylines - including the famous (or infamous, depending on your view) occasion when he was revealed as Vince McMahon's illegitimate son, and a period when he was the mascot for Degeneration X. On the pre-show of Extreme Rules in 2014 he had a hardcore match against fellow little wrestler El Torito where he was able to show off his in-ring ability, although the match was called 'WeeLC' and featured little people impersonating the commentary team, under the names 'Micro Cole', 'Jerry Smaller' and 'J-B-Elf'. Postl later described the match as the best he had in almost a decade with the company prior to his release in 2016, after which he continued to be active elsewhere in the industry: as well as multiple indie bookings he has had a couple of runs in Impact Wrestling and even a cameo on AEW Dynamite in late 2020.

In the past few years the debate about little people wrestling has flared up on several occasions, including in the UK. A Texas promotion called Extreme Dwarfanators Wrestling promoted a tour of England and Wales in 2018, sparking an angry response from a charity called the Restricted Growth Association (RGA), who called the events a "freak show" and asked venues that were hosting the tour to reconsider their involvement. The promotion responded by taking legal action, saying that the charity was discriminating against them, and eventually the tour went ahead. The row gained significant media coverage, including a fascinating argument on breakfast television show Good Morning Britain, which invited one of the wrestlers and the vice-chair of the RGA to debate the issue live. The discussion, which you can watch on YouTube, quite neatly encapsulates the two sides of the argument: wrestler Derec 'Little Riddle' Pemberton says that he doesn't feel demeaned by participating in the show and actively enjoys his work, so believes that he should be free to perform as he pleases. Meanwhile the RGA's Eugene Grant argues that even if the wrestlers in the show are happy to perform, their show perpetuates a stereotype that causes harm to the rest of the dwarfism community. The debate was not settled on that day, and the wider discussion about how little people are featured in the entertainment industry seems destined to be a hot topic of conversation for a long while to come.

EUGENE: EMPOWERMENT OR EXPLOITATION?

Perhaps the most notorious example of a wrestling character being portrayed as having developmental disabilities emerged in WWE during 2004. Nick Dinsmore, a talented wrestler who had spent several years stuck in developmental territory Ohio Valley Wrestling, had become frustrated by his lack of progress and was threatening to leave for a career competing in Japan. Soon after making his intentions known, he found himself in a meeting with Vince McMahon who explained that he was looking to find some good new characters for WWE television. Thinking on his feet, Dinsmore pitched an idea that had been suggested to him by OVW trainer Rip Rogers but had been rejected by various WWE agents when Dinsmore had suggested it to them in the past. He later explained in an interview: "*Rip came to me and [suggested] a wrestler who isn't very social, can't tie his shoes, and isn't very good in conversations but the minute he gets in the ring he can do all the moves flawlessly. He's an encyclopaedia of wrestling.*"

McMahon liked the idea, and within weeks Dinsmore found himself debuting on Monday Night Raw as Eugene, the 'special' nephew of general manager Eric Bischoff. Although not explicitly described as having a particular condition, the character displayed behaviours that are commonly seen among those on the autistic spectrum including 'stimming', which involves repetitive physical movements such as arm or hand-flapping, spinning, jumping or rocking. Bischoff placed Eugene under the supervision of William Regal, who immediately managed to lose him. Eugene had headed out into the arena to meet commentators Jim Ross and Jerry Lawler, deciding to lick a disgusted Lawler's head as a homage to the Bushwhackers. Two weeks later he was back in the ring, firing t-shirts into the crowd from a cannon and 'inadvertently' hitting Regal in the groin with one.

Regal initially resented having to keep his unpredictable new protégé in check, and was happy to oblige when Bischoff asked him to ensure that his nephew lost his debut match against Rob Conway - but it turned out that Eugene was a gifted wrestler and won the match anyway. The next week Bischoff's henchman Jonathan Coachman tried to verbally humiliate him in an in-ring promo so that he would no longer want to pursue his dream of being a wrestler but was remarkably interrupted by The Rock, who made his first appearance for the company since that year's Wrestlemania XX to defend the newcomer and give him the 'rub' of being in the ring with a bona fide star. Eugene's rise to being a featured character on Raw was complete, just six weeks after he first appeared on screen.

"*It was a comedy act at its core*," Bischoff said of Eugene on an episode of his podcast in 2022. "*It was meant to be light-hearted, entertaining, non-serious.*" But is that all it was, or did it cross the line into making fun of a disability for the sake of entertainment? Bischoff has come to believe the latter. "*I've learned in recent years that the things you do on television... can either really positively impact people or things that hurt people, and you don't really realise you're doing it,*" he said. "*What I didn't understand is that a lot of those things we did on television impacted the audience in ways that I would have never anticipated at that time. So now when I look back at that character, I think about parents who had kids with learning disabilities and who liked wrestling, and whose child liked wrestling - but here we were, having fun with that. It bothers me a little bit that I was part of that.*"

Perhaps there's an argument that the character would have been acceptable if he was portrayed as ultimately being an inspirational figure who overcomes the odds to achieve his dream - and at times, that was indeed the general thrust of Eugene's storyline arc. By November of his first year, he and Regal had won the world tag team titles and there were several times where he gave the company's various villains their comeuppance. Still, the problem for some was that there were other times when his entire purpose on a show seemed to be as comic relief with laughs generated by his disability. In other storylines his likeability was used simply as a way to get heat on some of the company's top bad guys: a case in point is his feud with Triple H during the summer of 2004, which resulted in The Game beating him at Summer-Slam. Eugene temporarily got revenge a fortnight later on Raw with a win assisted by Randy Orton, but the following week Triple H left his rival beaten and bloodied in a steel cage match to end their feud. So much for fairy tales.

Arguably worse still was the fact that by late 2006 the character had run out of steam so was booked to turn heel, at which point he was portrayed as having uncontrollable rage - it was hard to deny at this stage that a disability was being used to draw a heel reaction. The heel turn was dropped within a few weeks, and Eugene's days in the company were numbered - he was released the following year. But almost two decades later opinions are still split on his legacy: was he a bold attempt at a character that would inspire fans with developmental disabilities, a nasty example of the wrestling business exploiting difference to get a reaction, or simply a source of harmless, light-hearted entertainment?

A ONE-LEGGED MAN IN AN ASS-KICKING CONTEST

For those who lived through it, it's hard to forget the episode of Smackdown where we first got to see Zach Gowen wrestle.

Having appeared on Smackdown in May 2003 as a one-legged 'fan' in the crowd who became an ally of Hulk Hogan's masked alias Mr America, Gowen had drawn the ire of the evil Mr McMahon and, a few weeks later, was placed in a handicap alongside Stephanie McMahon against the giant Big Show with the promise of a WWE contract if he could defy the odds. As the match progressed, Gowen's prosthetic was removed and we got to see what he could do - athletically moving around the ring and hitting spectacular moves despite his disability, and ultimately landing a one-legged moonsault from the top rope to secure the victory. It was unlike anything that most of the audience had ever seen.

Gowen's road to that moment had been a long one. Growing up in Michigan, he was diagnosed with cancer and had his left leg amputated at the age of eight. He recovered from the disease and trained to be a pro wrestler, eventually appearing on an early TNA pay-per-view at the age of 19. WWE officials saw that appearance and made enquiries about signing him (in fact, director of talent relations John Laurinaitis reportedly signed the wrong one-legged wrestler at first in a case of mistaken identity, but that's another story), resulting in him making his debut just months later.

After that initial victory, McMahon's character continued to torment Gowen and the two eventually clashed at the Vengeance pay-per-view on 27th July 2003. The previous night the company aired a video package on its 'behind-the-scenes' show WWE Confidential, with interviews from Zach's family and friends telling his inspirational story. This was in sharp contrast to McMahon, who was saying some truly shocking things in order to draw the ire of fans: "*You may have survived cancer*," he told his opponent. "*You won't survive me.*" McMahon narrowly won the pay-per-view match but Gowen was portrayed as a valiant underdog who got an ovation from the crowd afterwards. Still, it felt a little bit flat: after all the effort that had been poured into telling the inspirational story of the protagonist and having the antagonist cross lines that made some viewers uncomfortable, the resolution was that the bad guy won?

A few weeks later WWE doubled down on using Gowen as a villain's victim, in a segment that is still among the most uncomfortable to watch in company history. Zach was placed in a match against Brock Lesnar in his hometown of Detroit, and the Beast wasted no time in beating him to a pulp in front of his mother and brother, 'breaking' his remaining leg and attacking him again while he was being stretchered away. Two weeks later, with Gowen in a wheelchair, a Smackdown segment saw Lesnar push him down a flight of stairs to rub more salt in the wound. Gowen spent a few weeks off television to sell the injury, and then returned to feud with Matt Hardy. Much like McMahon had before, Hardy mocked Gowen's disability during their feud, acting as guest commentator during a couple of his matches and dropping lines like "*I may be going out on a limb here - one limb specifically*" and "*everyone knows that Matt Hardy's career has more legs left in it than Zach Gowen's*". Still, at least this time Gowen had the last laugh with a singles victory at No Mercy. It was not long afterwards that a real-life injury put him on the shelf, and he was released from the company before he ever made his return, having struggled by his own admission to fit in with others in the locker room at such a young age.

Gowen continued to wrestle for several years afterwards on the independent scene, including a spell tagging as one half of the 'Handicapped Heroes' alongside Gregory Iron, a veteran of the scene who has carved out a great career as a wrestler despite suffering from cerebral palsy. Now semi-retired, Gowen now works as a motivational speaker and is kept busy as a father, but most fans remember him for that brief spell in WWE. On one level his story was inspirational, given all of the obstacles that he overcame, but some have argued that his story was presented as another example of an 'oddity' that simply gave viewers a chance to gawp at disability. As with Eugene and other examples mentioned in this story, Gowen's disability was eventually used as a means for heels to mock him. Both at the time and in the years since, some have found that offensive, whereas others think that Gowen's run in WWE was - at least to begin with - among the better executed depictions of a competitor with a disability.

SCARS AS A SHORTHAND FOR VILLAINY

Have you ever stopped to think about how many 'baddies' - not just in wrestling but throughout the entertainment industry - have a scar or other visible difference? The Joker in Batman, Scar in the Lion King, Darth Vader in Star Wars - the list goes on and on. According to a 2017 study by the University of Texas, six of the all-time top 10 movie villains (as identified by the American Film Institute) had scars, burns or other visible differences to their skin while none of the top 10 heroes had any such features.

Wrestling has not historically escaped this trend, and in fact has sometimes gone beyond using scarring as a shorthand for villainy - at times it has felt, much in the same way as how little people have been portrayed, that wrestling has used a performer's physical appearance as a source of spectacle, like in the 'freak shows' of the Victorian age. Take for example the portrayal of Kane when he first unmasked after more than five years of shielding his face because of its (storyline) disfigurement in a fire. At the end of the 23rd June 2003 episode of Raw, the 'Big Red Monster' is forced to show his true self after losing in the main event. As the big reveal took place, showing a face with blackened marks across it, the commentators yelled "*Is that a human?*" and "*Look at that grotesque face!*", while Kane himself was seemingly so trauma-tised by the shame of showing what he looked like that he spent the next several weeks on a violent rampage.

I (Adam) am a lifelong wrestling fan, but I'm also someone who has had to deal with lifelong neurofibromatosis, a genetic condition that caused large tumours to start devel-oping on my face when I was a young child. I've needed dozens of operations to help manage the issue, and also found that going to school was sometimes a harrowing experience. As a kid I got called names like 'Scarface', 'Two-Face' and 'Elephant Man' and - much like many other people with visible difference, I regularly saw villains on TV who had conditions similar to mine, but rarely if ever did I see someone with scarring portrayed as the hero of a story. With that having been my experience throughout my life, the presentation of Kane at that point sat uncomfortably with me then and continues to do so today. Like the rest of the entertainment industry, wrestling has long had a tendency to commodify disfigurement as being a source of difference and therefore a source of evil, much in the same way that women were promoted as being sex objects rather than talented wrestlers for so many years.

In fact, one of the worst examples from WWE combined the two: a beautiful woman who also had a facial disfigure-ment. Jillian Hall was brought onto the Smackdown roster in 2005 as a 'fixer' for the tag team MNM and later as an image consultant for John 'Bradshaw' Layfield. She had a large growth on the left side of her face, which everyone involved immediately treated as being disgusting - and it was regularly used as a source of comedy until eventually it was 'bitten off' by the Boogeyman. Seriously. It was one of the more egre-gious examples of a visible difference being used to belittle and mock.

In recent years I've been fortunate to work as an ambas-sador for a UK-based charity that is working to change perceptions. Changing Faces provides support and education to help improve the lives of people with visible differences, and in 2018 it launched a campaign entitled 'I Am Not Your Villain', which has been encouraging the entertainment industry to think more carefully about the effect that the practice of presenting visible difference as a shorthand for villainy has on people with visible differences in the real world. We're not asking for a blanket ban on villains with scars or marks – having that as a goal would be economically naive and foolish. Instead, we want to help bring about a cultural change across the film industry so that there is more balance in how people with visible difference are portrayed. It's the kind of progress that will only be made if people on all sides of the debate listen to each other and try to understand each other's points of view - for example, in wrestling's case I know that some people will think that examples such as Kane and Jillian Hall were harmless entertainment. Our goal is not to preach at you that you're a bad person for having watched and enjoyed those storylines but rather to get everyone thinking about the impact such portrayals have on others. In much the same way that the presentation of women has moved on leaps and bounds in recent years within the industry, the representation of people with disability or visible difference can do the same. We can all do better if we work together.

TOTAL DEVASTATION (CHRIS BENOIT #1)

Issue 43, July 2022

Dave Bradshaw

Sixteen years ago an unspeakable tragedy threatened the very existence of WWE. In the first half of a two-part article, Dave Bradshaw remembers the wreckage left behind by the Chris Benoit murder-suicide of June 2007...

I'll never, ever forget the moment the news broke. Much like people always talk about where they were when 9/11 happened or Princess Diana died, wrestling fans who lived through the night of Monday 25th June 2007 have it seared into their memories. In my case, it was the front room of my parents' house: I can't recall why I wasn't at my own flat or why on Earth I was still awake at that time, but I remember realising that it was almost 1am and deciding to flick over to Sky Sports to catch the start of the live Monday Night Raw broadcast before going to bed. I did so despite expecting that it would instantly annoy me, because after 16 years as a WWE fan I had never been as angry at its product as I had been in the previous two weeks.

After Vince McMahon's character had "died" in an exploding limousine (don't ask) at the end of Raw on 11th June, the Smackdown episode that week was dedicated to his memory and featured a ten-bell salute at the beginning with the roster looking solemn on the entrance stage. It then proceeded with heartfelt "tributes" from wrestlers and employees throughout the show, striking a tone offensively reminiscent of the genuine tribute shows it had presented to Owen Hart and Eddie Guerrero in recent years. If this didn't feel tasteless enough, the show took place on the same day that another beloved wrestling personality passed away for real: legendary wrestler and valet Sherri Martel was found dead that day of a drug overdose at her mother's home in Alabama. When I looked online the following day, I had to scroll down before I found any mention of her on the WWE.com homepage, buried beneath a huge banner head-line commemorating the totally fictional passing of Vincent Kennedy McMahon.

I was only half watching ten nights later as Raw began, busy staring at my phone and only briefly glancing at the screen to see one of the "In Memory Of" graphics that the company always used to flash at the start of the show when someone had legitimately died. I started to roll my eyes, assuming that this was the latest insult to the real life tragedies that this hokey McMahon storyline was mimicking - but then suddenly I did a double take and stood bolt upright with my hand across my mouth in disbelief. That wasn't Vince McMahon's photo on the graphic. It was Chris Benoit.

Suddenly I was looking at a wide shot of a totally empty arena, save for one man standing in the middle of the ring. It was Vince, looking very much alive but with the weight of the world on his shoulders. "*Good evening,*" he began. "*Tonight this arena here in Corpus Christi, Texas, was to have been filled to capacity with enthusiastic WWE fans. Tonight's storyline was to have been the alleged demise of my character, Mr McMahon. However, in reality, WWE superstar Chris Benoit, his wife Nancy and their son Daniel are dead. Their bodies were discovered this afternoon in their new suburban Atlanta home.*"

I remember that all the resentment I had been feeling

towards the man on my screen instantly melted away - in fact, I almost felt sorry for him. McMahon was clearly making one of the most difficult statements of his life and trying to piece things together just as much as I was, and presumably millions of other minds around the world were racing equally fast in that moment. What on Earth could have happened? Was it carbon monoxide poisoning? Had an intruder broken into their home and killed them all? Was this all just a bad dream? Never for a second did I imagine the version of events that turned out to be the truth, and in that moment it was clear that almost none of those who actually knew and worked with Benoit did either. *"Tonight will be a three-hour tribute to one of the greatest WWE superstars of all time,"* continued McMahon, his voice cracking with emotion. *"Tonight will be a tribute to Chris Benoit."* Cue a poignant tribute video set to 'One Thing', a rock ballad by the band Finger Eleven that still takes many of us back to that moment if we hear its opening chords.

The programme that followed felt at the time like a wonderful tribute and a perfect reminder of why WWE should never have parodied their own memorial shows in the weeks prior - they have the ability to handle real-world tragedies with great tact and grace when required, and appeared to have dealt with this moment expertly. The choice to cancel the live show was surely the right one, especially after the criticism they had received for their "show must go on" response to Owen Hart's death eight years earlier; the decision to immediately abandon the awful McMahon death storyline was very welcome; and going ahead with a three-hour Benoit tribute still seems understandable in hindsight, because barely anyone seemed to have any inkling at that point as to what horrors had really unfolded. The word "barely" is important there, however, because one person who spoke that night seemed strangely wary of heaping praise on the friend he had just lost. *"At a later date I'll be quite happy to sit here and tell you all the things about Chris Benoit that I'd like to tell you*," William Regal said softly into the camera. "*But now all I'm willing to say is that Chris Benoit was undoubtedly the hardest-working man in professional wrestling; the most dedicated and totally absorbed in the business of professional wrestling, more than anyone I've ever met. And that's really all I have to say at the moment - he was the absolute best. Thanks.*" It was brief, very guarded, and made no reference to Benoit's qualities as a person. Soon enough we would all understand why.

In fact, police in Georgia were already pretty confident of what had happened several hours before Raw started. The first hint that something was wrong had come on Saturday when Benoit missed a house show in Beaumont, Texas - he was known as a consummate professional who lived for his work and saw missing any dates as a serious failing. When WWE staff and fellow wrestlers contacted him that day he claimed that his wife Nancy and son Daniel had come down with severe food poisoning, but that he would join the crew in Houston for the next day's pay-per-view. When he failed to show up on Sunday alarm bells really started ringing, not least because of some odd text messages he had sent to wrestler Chavo Guerrero and referee Scott Armstrong in the early hours of that morning, including one providing the address of his house and another saying "*The dogs are in the enclosed pool area. Garage side door is open.*" By late Monday morning a WWE representative had called the local authorities asking if they could go to the house and check on Benoit's welfare. Upon arrival they recruited the woman who lived next door to climb over the fence for them because the two German shepherds guarding the property knew her and would not attack her. The neighbour entered the property and ran out screaming moments later, having found the bodies of Nancy and Daniel in separate rooms with copies of the Bible placed next to each of them. Police officers then entered and found Chris dead in the basement, after which they started piecing together what had happened.

THE COMING STORM

By the final hour of the Raw tribute to Benoit, some media outlets were starting to get wind of the fact that police were treating the deaths as a double murder and a suicide. Fox 5 News in Atlanta are believed to have been among the first to report this, and by Tuesday the harrowing truth had become apparent. At a press conference outside the house, police investigators confirmed their belief that Chris strangled Nancy on the Friday night, suffocated Daniel at some point early on Saturday, and hanged himself with the cord from a weight machine in his home gym on Sunday morning. It was a tale so unfathomably macabre that it was hard to process but impossible to stop thinking about, the kind of crime that would make even the most world-weary among us shake our heads in disgust and despair. But the moment those lurid details were revealed to the world, it was also the beginning of something else - the first bolt of lightning in a storm that would quickly become so ferocious that it would threaten to rip down the entire WWE house.

On Tuesday evening it was clear that Vince McMahon had realised just how dark the gathering clouds were. WWE was in the middle of its ill-fated ECW revival at the time (in fact, Benoit had been scheduled to win the ECW title on the pay-per-view he had missed two days earlier), and its weekly show aired that night. It began with McMahon standing in a studio speaking into the camera, but he had a very different message to the one he had delivered the previous night. "*Last night on Monday Night Raw the WWE presented a special tribute show recognising the career of Chris Benoit*," he began. "*However, now*

some 26 hours later the facts of this horrific tragedy are now appar-
ent. Therefore, other than my comments there will be no mention of
Mr Benoit's name tonight. On the contrary, tonight's show will be
dedicated to everyone who has been affected by this terrible incident.
This evening marks the first step of the healing process. Tonight,
WWE performers will do what they do better than anyone else in the
world: entertain you." He wasn't kidding about there being no
mention of Benoit's name - in fact, in the decade and a half
since that 30-second speech there has barely been a single
utterance of the name "Benoit" on WWE television. But the
second part of the message was equally clear: by saying that
his performers would help start the healing process
McMahon was trying to position WWE as the solution, not
the problem. He understood the existential threat that was
coming, and he was already in survival mode.

The media frenzy began immediately. For much of the
next fortnight the endless cycle of cable news seemed to talk
about little else: CNN, Fox News and MSNBC were all
camped outside the Benoit house for live coverage on their
shows during the day, before their primetime hosts debated
what had happened each evening with panels of former
wrestlers, criminal psychologists and medical experts. It was a
level of mainstream attention that WWE would have craved
under normal circumstances, but of course this was anything
but normal and the attention was anything but positive.
Almost immediately the main subject of debate seemed to be
steroids, and whether Benoit might have killed his wife and
child in a fit of "roid rage". The police had found testosterone
in the house, along with painkillers, tranquilisers, growth
hormone, antidepressants and numerous other prescription
drugs - but of these it was the steroids that seemed to provide
the most attractive hook for news coverage. One of the only
other times that WWE (then WWF) had attracted such
attention form news media was 13 years earlier when
McMahon stood trial on charges of supplying his wrestlers

with steroids, and although he was acquitted, the stereotype of pro wrestlers as chemically-enhanced musclemen had endured for those who usually don't pay attention to the industry. That's not to say that pro wrestling didn't still have a steroid problem in 2007, but the notion that steroids were the main culprit in the Benoit tragedy was only one theory among many - a simplistic story that could provoke fiery television debate but produced far more heat than light. The return of such a discussion to the airwaves must have felt to McMahon like his worst nightmare, dredging up the same kinds of allegations that had caused the WWF brand so much reputational damage in 1994.

The sudden media rush to find people from the wrestling industry they could use as contributors for their broadcasts and articles meant that a seemingly endless stream of well-known wrestling names were given airtime and column inches, plenty of whom did not have complimentary things to say about the McMahon empire. *"If the head of the organisation is known to be a steroid user like that, can anyone believe the inside drug testing that the organisation does?"* former world champion Bruno Sammartino said of Vince McMahon in one interview. *"I find it extremely difficult for anybody to take that seriously."* Another world champion, Lex Luger, told several media outlets about the havoc that steroids had wreaked in his own life and said it was impossible to rule out that they played a role in the Benoit murders. Debra Marshall, the former WWE manager and ex-wife of 'Stone Cold' Steve Austin, told Sean Hannity of Fox News that steroids had caused her ex-husband to have panic attacks and to violently attack her. Marc Mero, who wrestled for both the WWF and WCW during his career in the 1990s, appeared on numerous shows to talk about the scandal of premature deaths among wrestlers and his belief that steroids were a major contributing factor. The procession of negative testimonies seemed endless - McMahon might have aimed to quickly stem the bleeding with his statement on ECW the night after news of the tragedy had broken, but as June turned into July his company seemed like it might die a death by a thousand cuts.

Indeed, despite the focus on steroids, the forensic spotlight that was cast on the pro wrestling industry and WWE in particular meant that the conversation soon strayed to other subjects that were equally uncomfortable territory. That question of premature deaths in the industry entered the public consciousness to a degree that it never had before, as did issues like drug and alcohol abuse, painkiller addiction, and the damaging effects on wrestlers' family lives from being on the road for up to 300 days each year. From there some discussions asked why wrestlers didn't feel like they could request downtime if they were hurt, and logically the subject then turned to questions like why wrestlers were treated as independent contractors rather than employees, what that meant for them in terms of lacking health benefits or other protections, and why they didn't unionise to get themselves a better deal. There was also detailed scrutiny of the company's drug testing policy that had been introduced in 2006, with questions being continuously raised about its effectiveness and its independence. It goes without saying that WWE executives would surely rather these discussions were not being played out every night on prime time television, but some who followed the business sensed a moment of reckoning and wondered if the awful events in the Benoit house might prove to be a catalyst for lasting change in an industry that had managed to avoid serious oversight for decades.

At times, WWE didn't exactly help its own case with its response to the ongoing furore. On that Tuesday as the authorities revealed that steroids had been found in the house, the company quickly released a statement saying that steroids *"were not and could not be related to the cause of death"*, despite the facts of the case being far from established and the results of toxicology reports still being weeks away. Two mornings later on Thursday 28th June, McMahon himself appeared on NBC's Today programme and seemed rattled when asked how his organisation had been able to reach such a definitive conclusion so rapidly. "*We didn't say that,*" he initially claimed when presented with the quote, before he was challenged on it again and tried to clarify that it was a response specifically to the claim that a "rage" had caused Benoit's actions. Later in the interview he was confronted with a statistic about the high number of wrestlers who had died at a young age, to which his response was that only five individuals had died while under contract - Benoit by suicide, Owen Hart by accident, and three others by heart failure. To some viewers the implication seemed to be that WWE was absolving itself of any connection with wrestlers who died prematurely unless the deceased person happened to be working for them at the time that he or she passed away. It was a moment when the company might have benefited from showing humility and a willingness to listen, but instead it sometimes struck a tone that was decidedly combative.

SEARCHING FOR ANSWERS

If further evidence was needed that WWE was not winning the public relations war, it arrived on 6th July when it became clear that public anger about the tragedy had pushed the nation's politicians into action. Cliff Stearns, a Republican congressman from Florida, called for a formal investigation into steroid use in professional wrestling. "*[The] abnormally high number of deaths of young, fit athletes should raise congressional alarms,*" read a press release from Stearns' office. "*Millions of young wrestling fans, for better or for worse, look up to professional wrestlers as role models. The Anabolic Steroid Act of*

1990 makes it a felony to use and distribute these drugs. Congress needs to investigate the recent events and find out how big of a problem steroid use is in professional wrestling." The stakes had been raised again: now WWE wasn't just battling negative publicity but also faced scrutiny and perhaps even sanctions from the federal government itself. Importantly though, the focus was only on steroids, meaning that some of the other thorny topics raised during those weeks about wrestler welfare and employment status seemed destined to fall by the wayside.

Meanwhile, another possible factor in Benoit's actions was coming into focus courtesy of a very credible source. Chris Nowinski was a Harvard graduate who played American football in college and went on to compete as a WWE wrestler in 2002 and 2003, before persistent symptoms of post-concussion syndrome forced him into retirement. He then dedicated his professional life to studying the type of brain injury that had affected him, gaining a PhD in behavioural neuroscience from Boston University and publishing a book in 2006 about the problem of concussions in the NFL. A number of American footballers had died in recent years after showing signs of unusual behaviour, and Nowinski believed they had been affected by chronic traumatic encephalopathy (CTE), a neurodegenerative disease caused by repeated trauma to the head. Nowinski reached out to Benoit's father four days after the murder-suicide and gained permission for a team at Boston University to examine his son's brain. The findings were shocking: Benoit had brain damage equivalent to that of an elderly person in the advanced stages of Alzheimer's disease. Of course, that alone could not explain Benoit's murderous behaviour any more than the toxicology results (which did eventually provide evidence of steroids in Benoit's system) could definitively say that steroids were the cause. Still, the findings added to the sense that this case was much more complex than was suggested by media coverage in the immediate aftermath of the tragedy.

Not every suggested factor that might have contributed to the tragedy was physical. Some pointed to Benoit's personality, or at least to how it changed after the death of his close friend Eddie Guerrero in 2005. That loss, along with the deaths of some other important people in his life at around the same time, seemed to send Benoit into an emotional downward spiral from which he never fully recovered. A few of his peers have also pointed to hints of a hidden side to Benoit that had always stayed beneath the surface. Sean 'X-Pac' Waltman said in a 2014 interview that he *"was a pleasant guy, but always had a darkness about him ... a sadness, or something,"* and that he had an odd sense of humour, finding amusement in *"things that were a little bit bent."* There was also some prior evidence of alleged violence in the relationship between Chris and Nancy: numerous accounts have said that their partnership was volatile, and Nancy even filed for divorce in 2003 after claiming that Chris had lost his temper and threatened to hit her during a row in April that year. They eventually made amends and got back together four months later.

Mostly, though, the testimonies about Chris Benoit from those who knew him best painted a picture of a quiet, intense, but ultimately good person. 'Stone Cold' Steve Austin described him after his death as *"one of the nicest guys I ever met in my life"*; John Cena called him the type of guy you want to go to war with; Edge described how Benoit had helped him through difficult times in his personal life; Bret Hart and Chris Jericho both gave glowing character references during a discussion about the tragedy on CNN's Larry King Live. There were anecdotes about Benoit's old-school wrestling values and how he used to punish himself by doing squats in the locker room if he made a mistake in the ring; about how he idolised the legendary English wrestler Tom 'Dynamite Kid' Billington and sought to emulate his style;

about his almost obsessive dedication to achieving excellence as a pro wrestler; about his devotion to his youngest son, whom he sometimes brought backstage to live events. All were fascinating insights, but none gave any obvious clues that he had it in him to do what he did to his own family. If anything those accounts only add to the mystery of how he could ever have committed such an unspeakable atrocity.

In the end it was a mystery that could never be totally solved, and the public appetite for action in response to the tragedy eventually diminished. Even the worst storms eventually pass, and the nature of the news cycle meant that the awful story of the Benoit family was soon pushed to the side, only occasionally bubbling back to the surface if new information such as the toxicology reports allowed cable news to squeeze a couple more hours of content from it. The political interest in addressing steroid use in the industry was soon overshadowed by the more high profile issue of steroids in professional baseball, and by the end of 2007 it was pretty clear that there would be no major action from the government in response to what had happened. It may, however, come to be seen as the moment that finally heralded a shift in the lifestyle and culture of professional wrestling locker rooms. As we will see in the second part of this article, it also led to improvements in WWE's drug-testing programme, its concussion protocols, and the steps it took to protect the welfare of its talent. In the end those changes were made on WWE's terms rather than being forced by legislation or fan pressure, but company executives surely knew that for a brief moment in 2007 there was a possibility of the industry being changed from the outside in ways that they would not be able to control, and on a purely human level the tragedy was something that no-one involved in the industry could bear to ever see duplicated. Changes had to be made, and soon enough they would be.

Three years before the events of June 2007, Chris Benoit

had stood in the middle of the ring at Madison Square Garden as confetti rained on him from the rafters, celebrating his capture of the World Heavyweight Championship in a classic main event at WrestleMania XX. Eddie Guerrero, who retained the company's other world championship on the same night, ran to the ring to embrace him. That moment, which would otherwise be considered among the most iconic in the history of the sport, now seems eerie to some and plain unwatchable to others - a testament to how fleeting life can be and how quickly things can change. But most of all if you watch it back now, the overriding feeling you might feel is a profound sadness. Benoit wasn't only joined by his best friend during that celebration but also by his wife and children, and got down on a knee to give a warm hug to the four-year-old son he seemed to adore. To think that the woman in that scene, who had been a pioneering figure in the wrestling industry in her own right, had her life so cruelly snatched away is heartbreaking on its own. To think that the innocent little boy hugging his father in that ring would also soon be killed by him seems - even now, all this time later - to be so far beyond the pale that there are no words to adequately describe it. It is a void that can never be filled, however much positive change it would eventually create...

FROM THE ASHES (CHRIS BENOIT #2)

Issue 44, August 2022.

Dave Bradshaw

In the second instalment of a two-part article to mark the 16-year anniversary of the Benoit family tragedy, Dave Bradshaw explores how positive change somehow emerged from professional wrestling's darkest hour...

It might seem like hyperbole to say it 15 years later, with WWE still an entertainment juggernaut and turning a handsome profit for its shareholders every year, but by July of 2007 there really was a feeling that Vince McMahon's empire was facing its gravest threat. The almost unmentionable evil of what must have transpired over that infamous weekend, where Chris Benoit murdered his wife Nancy and seven-year-old son Daniel in their home before killing himself, was felt so viscerally by everyone who heard about it that it seemed like a natural human reaction to say "something must be done". Wrestling fans wanted it, talking heads on television news demanded it, and it even seemed to focus the minds of politicians for a short while.

But what was "it", exactly? It was one thing to agree that something awful had happened and that it must never happen again, but it was quite another to reach any kind of consensus on the causes of the catastrophe, let alone the solutions. The

WWE's public statements that summer seemed determined to place the blame solely on the individual: the cause was that Chris Benoit was simply an anomaly; a deranged monster who could have been working in any industry but happened to be working in theirs. Meanwhile, for much of the mainstream news media the cause was assumed to be "roid rage", the phenomenon whereby people taking anabolic steroids can suddenly explode into uncontrollable fits of violent anger. For the more knowledgeable wrestling media, a much more complex list of factors may have contributed, including the mental and physical consequences of WWE's gruelling schedule, a locker room culture that did little to help, and the unresolved grief of Benoit losing some of his closest friends. And then there were the causes suggested by those with medical expertise, in particular the work of former WWE wrestler Chris Nowinski and his colleagues at Boston University who examined the effects of multiple concussions on Benoit's brain and concluded that he had damage equivalent to a patient with advanced Alzheimer's Disease.

With so many conflicting takes on the situation, no-one could give a definitive account of what could or should happen next - but some of the change that happened immediately was inevitable. From the moment Vince McMahon declared "*there will be no mention of Mr Benoit's name tonight*" at the start of a WWE broadcast the day after the bodies had been discovered and it had become apparent that Benoit himself was the culprit, his existence was essentially scrubbed from WWE canon. This was no mean feat given the central role he played as an on-screen character during the previous seven years - especially in 2004 when he won the Royal Rumble as the first entrant, claimed the world title in the iconic closing scene of WrestleMania XX at Madison Square Garden, and took the fall that made Randy Orton the youngest world champion in company history at SummerSlam.

Two years after the tragedy it actually seemed as though Vince McMahon's position on this subject might have been softening: in an interview with a one-off WWE magazine called *The Untold History of the WWE* he was asked by a reader about the subject and responded: "*It's not right to pretend he [Benoit] didn't exist. It's one thing to include him as part of a historical perspective, which I believe is OK, and it's another thing to promote him, which is not OK. The situation is very similar to that of O.J. Simpson - despite his controversy. O.J. was still part of the NFL scene. You can't deny that he existed.*"

Ultimately though, WWE's definition of what counts as "promoting" his role proved to be quite wide-ranging - when the WWE Network launched in 2014 and made its back catalogue of pay-per-views and TV shows available to stream, Benoit's matches were not deleted but his name was not searchable. To this day, if you search for his SummerSlam match against Orton it is listed as "Randy Orton challenges for the world title" rather than "Randy Orton vs Chris Benoit", like a match against any other opponent would be. Company-produced documentaries continue to carefully edit around any archive footage of Benoit, and WWE talent has reportedly been banned from mentioning his name in interviews. Some fans have argued that this is unfair, and a small number have even lobbied for Benoit to be inducted into the Hall of Fame for his in-ring contributions, but it seems harsh in the extreme to criticise the company for keeping their distance. Any perception that they were trying to profit from Benoit's name or to gloss over the gruesome final chapter of his life would surely result in a torrent of negative publicity and, more importantly, would be grossly insensitive to the loved ones of Nancy and Daniel.

LEARNING THE WRONG LESSONS?

WWE's strategy of pushing forwards without further acknowledgement of Benoit was probably therefore its only option, especially in the summer of 2007, and it proved to be an effective one. There was little the company could do in the immediate aftermath of the tragedy except to weather the storm of negative publicity and hope that the short attention span of the news cycle meant that the public's attention would soon move elsewhere. In the end that's exactly what happened, and with it went the will of politicians to exert much effort in investigating the industry and its practices. Early threats of congressional investigations had all but subsided by the end of the year, arguably giving McMahon a valuable lesson in how to deal with any future PR crisis. WWE hasn't faced anything else quite as serious as the Benoit fallout in the 15 years since, but there have been a few moments where the company has generated negative head-lines and its strategy almost always seems to have been to carry on regardless and have faith that the drama will only be temporary.

In the autumn of 2018 when other American corporations were pulling out of deals with the Saudi Arabian regime after the murder of journalist Jamal Khashoggi, Vince McMahon resisted pressure to withdraw from a lucrative agreement to stage a series of live shows in the kingdom over the next 10 years. Whatever the ethical merits of that choice, it looks in hindsight like a commercially savvy one: much like in 2007 after Benoit, the noise around the company died down soon enough, and the highly profitable partnership survived. Two years later as the US approached a political crossroads at its 2020 election, WWE was in the midst of a row with some of its talent about who should keep the profits when wrestlers monetised their likeness on platforms such as Twitch and

Cameo. A prominent Democrat named Andrew Yang responded to the controversy by vowing to investigate WWE's labour practices if Joe Biden became president, and his interest in the subject seemed more authentic than most previous threats that politicians had made towards the company. Undeterred, WWE pushed forward regardless with its insistence that it owned the image rights of all of its performers, and was apparently willing to gamble that Yang's proposed crackdown would never come to pass. As we now know, Biden did indeed win the election, but 18 months into the new administration Yang is yet to find himself in a position where he has been able to take meaningful action.

Fast forward another two years and Vince McMahon is embroiled in yet another crisis - this time being investigated by his own board of directors after allegedly paying a mistress $3 million to keep quiet about their extramarital affair. Although he has temporarily stepped down as company chairman, McMahon's overall approach to this latest predicament seems markedly similar to how he has behaved before when his back seems to be against the wall - he is still running the show creatively, and his bizarre appearance to open Smackdown on the Friday after the story broke felt like a public act of defiance towards those who might wish him ill. In this sense, then, you could make a case that an important lesson McMahon and WWE learned from the aftermath of the Benoit tragedy was that they should resist any urge to make knee jerk changes in how they conduct themselves when threatened with scrutiny, because those threats will almost always amount to nothing.

There might be some merit to this argument, but it also overlooks the fact that real, meaningful change has happened organically within WWE and the wider wrestling business over the past 15 years, without the need for it to be imposed on the industry by lawmakers. Among the arguments put forward by some wrestling journalists in 2007 as possible contributory factors in the deterioration of Benoit's health before he did the unthinkable was that he was a victim of a culture that had led to a disproportionately high number of premature deaths among professional wrestlers. It was a life in which the schedule was gruelling, performers sometimes felt pressure to work while hurt so that they wouldn't lose their prominent positions on the show, and many numbed the pain of their physical and mental problems through addiction to painkillers, alcohol or recreational drugs.

While those are all still undoubtedly problems to some extent in 2022, the general consensus among those who have been around the business for long enough to compare different eras seems to be that the men and women in today's WWE locker room behave in healthier ways than their predecessors, and are more likely to spend their spare time playing video games than indulging in more destructive personal habits. Bizarrely, some veterans appear nostalgic for the locker room culture of yesteryear, believing that the habits of the current generation of wrestlers make them somehow less tough than those who came before them. The Undertaker raised some eyebrows in 2021 when he appeared on The Joe Rogan Experience and said the current product was "kind of soft", adding: "*I remember walking into my first real dressing room, and all I saw were some crusty f***ing men. Half of them had guns and knives in their bags... Now you walk in, there's guys playing video games and f***ing making sure they look pretty. It's evolution, I guess. I don't know what it is, but I just like those eras, man. I liked when men were men.*" It was a statement that seemed to demonstrate how deeply entrenched those old-school attitudes were until the recent past, and just how much the culture has changed in a short space of time.

Things have gone even further on the independent scene, particularly in Europe. Bringing about changes that might improve working conditions for professional wrestlers, such as the ability to unionise, the provision of health insurance and other employment benefits, have proved to be intractable problems in the context of WWE and American labour laws, but real progress has been made elsewhere. For example, UK performers' union Equity now allows wrestlers to become members, meaning that in exchange for subscription fees of around £180 per year they can access legal assistance if promoters refuse to pay them money they are owed, receive compensation if they suffer a long-term injury that damages their ability to earn a living, and be indemnified against any accidental injury they might cause to other wrestlers or audience members. Some promotions have been working with the union too, particularly on things like codes of conduct, Dignity at Work policies and safeguarding measures to prevent abuse. While none of these developments are a direct consequence of the Benoit tragedy, most of them would have seemed inconceivable in 2007. They represent tangible progress, and are a sign of an industry that is slowly professionalising.

ALL IN THEIR HEADS

Within WWE itself, quite aside from a shift in the backstage culture, there have been some improvements to company policies that surely have been directly influenced by what happened in Benoit's case. One such example is the concussion protocol, which developed in part thanks to the company's close cooperation with Nowinski and his colleagues in the years after the tragedy. In 2013 the company announced it would donate $1.2 million to Nowinski's Sports Legacy Institute over the next three years to help fund research into Chronic Traumatic Encephalopathy (CTE), the condition from which Benoit is believed to have been suffering at the time of his heinous actions. In the same year that the donations were made, three high profile names on the company's main roster - Fandango, Christian and Dolph Ziggler - were all kept off television for long periods because they were suffering with the after-effects of concussions. During that same period the company quietly banned some moves that could cause damage to wrestlers' heads (or to kids at home who chose to imitate them) such as piledrivers and the Seth Rollins curb stomp, as well as issuing a total prohibition on chair shots to the head with fines and suspensions for anyone who disobeyed. According to WWE's corporate website, it also now provides an annual *"educational seminar for all talent, referees, producers & medical personnel that addresses the topics of... concussion awareness, the WWE protocols for treatment and the latest medical information regarding this area."*

In terms of testing its talent for signs of a problem, WWE's policy also seems very thorough. Every wrestler takes an "ImPACT test" when they join the company and subsequently once a year, which is *"a computerised neurocognitive assessment tool that measures the effects of a concussion through cognitive testing."* Anyone who then demonstrates symptoms of a concussion has to pass another ImPACT test, the results of which are examined by a qualified doctor, before they are allowed to return to action. These tests are administered within 48 hours of any physical symptoms of concussion disappearing, to see if the patient really has recovered. If they do not pass the test they are put through *"a graded exertion test to see if physical activity will retrigger the talents concussion symptoms"* and are only allowed to compete again if they also show no symptoms during that examination. In cases where the symptoms or test results are sufficiently severe, the talent in question can be sent to see a concussion specialist in Pittsburgh, and any talent who suffers two concussions within a year of each other is automatically sent there for a neuropsychological evaluation before they can get back to action. The thoroughness of this policy prompted GQ Magazine to say in

2016 that *"the WWE has ramped up its concussion protocol to the point where they are at the forefront of how head injuries are handled amongst all sport leagues."* The writers of that article pointed out that the company had recently held firm in its decision to keep top star Daniel Bryan benched indefinitely, even after multiple external doctors were prepared to clear him, because he was not reaching the high safety bar that the organisation had set for itself.

Indeed, concussion safety had now become a guiding principle from the very first stages of a new wrestler's training, especially since WWE took its developmental system fully in-house and opened its new Performance Center in 2013. According to a Bleacher Report story the following year, the company had already been insisting for some time that when trainees are learning the "flat back bump", one of the basics of how to fall safely in wrestling, that they must wear headgear and practice on crash mats until their technique is so good that it is deemed safe for them to try it on the harder surface of a wrestling ring canvas. The reason for this is that taking such a bump involves a whiplash motion that could cause a concussion if not done correctly. According to the report, the opening of the Performance Center further added to this push towards safety, as the facility included a "high-spot" ring where the canvas is actually a giant crash pad and one corner has a larger platform than the standard turnbuckle provides, so that *"both rookie and experienced wrestlers alike can get more acclimated to coming off the ropes or practice new moves, respectively, without any wear and tear on their bodies, whether musculoskeletal or neurological."*

While the company has undoubtedly been proactive in its approach to concussion safety during the past 15 years, that is not to say that it accepts responsibility for any brain damage alleged by those in the past or present who have competed for it. Three years after the Benoit tragedy when Linda McMahon's campaign for a US Senate seat led to another period of intense scrutiny for WWE, the company was careful not to accept any liability for his actions. During that election campaign Benoit's father Michael wrote an open letter to the Connecticut voters who would decide whether to elect Linda as their senator, claiming that she and Vince regarded their wrestlers as *"little more than circus animals to be ridden until their value expires."* There was an immediate political imperative for the company to deny this, given the consequences it could have had for Linda's electoral fortunes, but there was also a longer term legal dilemma involved. From the outside it felt like a difficult tightrope for the company to tread: on the one hand it was commendably starting to tighten up its procedures for talent who suffered from concussions, but on the other hand it seemed unable to concede that such changes were necessary because doing so might imply that it had had insufficient protections in place previously. Any acceptance of responsibility felt like an open invitation for someone from the company's past to file a lawsuit.

In the end, the lawsuit came anyway. Over 50 former in-ring competitors commenced legal action against the company in 2016, claiming damages because they said they had suffered brain damage as a result of the abuse their bodies had taken from repeatedly working in a WWE ring. Two years later the case was dismissed on the grounds that it could not be proved that the wrestlers' work with WWE had been the main cause of injury in most cases (most of them had also wrestled elsewhere, after all), nor could the company have reasonably known about the risks posed by concussions given the medical knowledge available at that time. The decision to find in favour of WWE was upheld on appeal in September 2020, and in April 2021 the US Supreme Court declined to take the case, meaning that the claimants had no more legal avenues to pursue.

· · ·

While the development of the concussion protocol has been broadly praised by those following the company, it is only one part of a larger "Talent Wellness Program" that has sometimes been the subject of heavy criticism. The program was first introduced in early 2006, shortly after the sudden death of WWE legend Eddie Guerrero, and has expanded its scope over time. The program's pages on the WWE website say that – in addition to the work already discussed around concussions – it also includes "cardiovascular testing, substance abuse and drug testing, annual physicals, and health care referrals." Of these, the issue of testing for banned substances has been the most controversial.

The basic premise of the testing system that WWE has developed is that all talent agree in their contracts to provide urine, blood, saliva and/or hair samples as requested as part of a regimen of random testing that will see everyone tested at least four times per year. The company is also allowed to test its talent if they have "reasonable suspicion" that they might have been consuming banned substances based on their symptoms and behaviours, or if they are caught in possession of any such substances. The list of prohibited items is extensive and includes anabolic steroids, muscle relaxers, sleep aids and recreational drugs, as well as medication unless the performer is in possession of a valid prescription. Alcohol is prohibited within 12 hours of a show, and any positive test for alcohol or cannabis results in a fine of $2,500. Positive tests for other substances on the list result in a "three-strike" scale of punishments: for the first offence there is a 30-day suspension without pay; for the second offence it's 60 days without pay; and a third strike results in the person being released from the company.

It all sounds quite thorough, but criticisms over the years

have centred around claims that the system is too easy to cheat and that it is not applied consistently to all talent. WWE reportedly only applies the policy to full-time talent, which could explain why Brock Lesnar was not affected when he failed a drugs test in UFC and was banned from that organisation for a year. Such a rule would also explain why people like Triple H and Vince McMahon may not have been subject to the same standards of testing as other on-air talent during these past 15 years – their prominent roles in the company have raised questions among some pundits and fellow wrestlers about whether they receive special treatment, and whether that rule about part-time talent might be in place to save them from having to participate in regular testing. While it's difficult to prove or disprove those kinds of accusations, it certainly isn't true more broadly to say that the policy is applied more leniently to the biggest stars whom the company cannot afford to lose from television for 30 or 60 days at a time. Randy Orton, Roman Reigns, Edge and Rey Mysterio have all been handed suspensions at various points while performing at or near the top of the card, so while the system might not be perfect it certainly isn't the sham that some have accused it of being.

In fact, it's probably accurate to say that the Wellness Program has saved lives. One of the clearest examples of this came from another element of the program in the months immediately following the Benoit tragedy and involved the man with whom he had been feuding on television that year. MVP, at that time the United States Champion, was found during a routine physical examination as part of the program to have an abnormality in his heart that could have led to sudden cardiac arrest while he was wrestling. Because the condition was caught before it caused a problem, it could be fixed and may well have prevented a tragedy. Meanwhile the company also launched a "Former Talent Drug and Alcohol Rehabilitation Assistance Program" in late 2007, providing help for any former talents that may have addictions or other substance abuse problems. The company reportedly sends out an annual letter to all former talent ensuring that they know about this service, and provides a confidential hotline for any of them who wish to seek admittance to a rehab centre, with all costs covered by WWE. While it's not clear that the provision of this offer came as a direct result of the Benoit situation, its arrival just three months later certainly raises questions as to whether the two were related.

None of this is to say that WWE's response to those awful events in June 2007 was flawless, and there are still plenty of the company's business practices for which it could plausibly be criticised. Nor is it to say that all of the positive changes in the past 15 years were a direct result of what happened to the Benoit family. Even if they were, they wouldn't make up for the profound loss that was suffered on that awful weekend. However, it feels important to acknowledge the areas where progress has been made, and there is genuine reason to believe that tragedies like the Benoit murder-suicide and all the other premature deaths of wrestlers from earlier generations might not be repeated on the same scale by those who are performing today. The story of the past 15 years in WWE and professional wrestling more generally might reasonably be defined as one of improvement - stuttering, uneven and sometimes frustratingly slow improvement, still punctuated from time to time with moments of shame or worse - but improvement nonetheless, of the sort that gives us reason to hope that in 2022 it is at least somewhat less likely that the industry will ever again be rocked by an event as harrowing as the horror that unfolded in an Atlanta suburb 15 years ago.

SOME OF THE BIGGEST WELLNESS POLICY
SUSPENSIONS SINCE 2006 (info courtesy of Fightful.com)

2006

Kurt Angle – Suspended for 30 days in June or July 2006. Left
for TNA Wrestling.
Rob Van Dam – Suspended for 30 days in July 2006. Pulled
over with marijuana and vicodin in his car.
Sabu – Fined $1,000 in July 2016 after being pulled over with
marijuana and vicodin in his car.
Randy Orton – Suspended for 30 days in August 2006

2007

Jeff Hardy – Suspended for 30 days in July 2007
Umaga – Suspended for 30 days on August 30, 2007
Booker T – Suspended for 60 days on August 30, 2007
Edge – Suspended for 30 days on August 30, 2007. Signature
Pharmacy scandal
John Morrison – Suspended for 30 days on August 30, 2007
Mr. Kennedy – Suspended for 30 days on August 30, 2007.
Signature Pharmacy scandal. Anastrozole, somatropin and
testosterone.
Chris Masters – Suspended for 60 days on November 2, 2007.
Released the following week.

2008

Jeff Hardy – Suspended for 60 days on March 11, 2008
William Regal – Suspended for 60 days on May 20, 2008
Dolph Ziggler – Suspended for 30 days on October 10, 2008

2009

Umaga – Released on June 8, 2009 for refusing rehab
Rey Mysterio – Suspended for 30 days in September, 2009.
Claims he was taking a prescription for his knee and arm

2010

Carlito – Contract terminated on May 21, 2010 for refusing
rehab after Wellness Policy violation.

2012

Evan Bourne – Suspended for 60 days on January 17, 2012.
Stated it was for Serenity Now synthetic marijuana.
Rey Mysterio – Suspended for 60 days on April 26, 2012
Randy Orton – Suspended for 60 days on May 30, 2012

2015

Hornswoggle – Suspended for 30 days on September 26, 2015.
Says he didn't provide a urine sample.

2016

Roman Reigns – Suspended for 30 days on June 21, 2016
Alberto Del Rio – Suspended for 30 days on August 17, 2016
Paige – Suspended for 30 days on August 17, 2016
Paige – Suspended for 60 days on October 10, 2016

2020

Andrade - Suspended for 30 days on January 27, 2020 while
United States Champion
Samoa Joe- Suspended for 30 days on February 24, 2020

CURTAIN OPEN

Issue 23, November 2020

Alex Whearity

It was once the corner stone of the entire industry. Yet in the past 25 years kayfabe has become a thing of the past, as numerous documentaries have now fully exposed once vaulted secrets of the wrestling business. Alex Whearity assessed the full impact of exposing the inner workings of the business and considered the lasting effect this has had on our viewing experience and our perception of the performers creating it.

Kayfabe: the practice of trying to make people believe that wrestlers are particular characters, when in fact they are only pretending to be those characters. (Cambridge Dictionary 2020)

December 28th, 1984, 20/20 reporter John Stossel infamously encounters 'Doctor Death' David Schultz backstage at Madison Square Garden. Stossel's objective? To expose the secrets of the wrestling business. A controversial figure famous for his belligerent style of questioning, Stossel steps up to David Schultz, who has been asked by Vince McMahon to speak with the reporter. Schultz, a man who has been raised on keeping the outward validity of the wrestling business intact is asked the question that all wrestlers and fans despise - *"I think wrestling is fake?"*. What followed was an incident that Vice's *Dark Side of the Ring* series termed 'The slap heard around the world'. Schultz slapped Stossel around the ear in response and then did it a second time for good measure. Stossel, in response, filed a lawsuit against WWF and received $425,000 in punitive damages. His investigation into the wrestling business not only got him a sore ear and a big rating for 20/20, but also put the microscope on how wrestling matches were really constructed.

Dark Side of the Ring covered this story magnificently, detailing how Schultz' actions on that night led to his termination from the WWF and an eventual career resurrection as a bounty hunter. The critically acclaimed *Dark Side of the Ring* documentary series has been one of Vice's premiere attractions and has dissected some of wrestling's most infamous characters and incidents. Creators of DSOTR, Evan Husney and Jason Eisener, have done a brilliant job with their research, with 87 different interviews for season two alone. The success of the show has been the truth that permeates from its core with honest, visceral stories of wrestlers and their families destroyed by an industry oxymoronically built on make believe. In season two the directors delved into murder (Chris Benoit), drug abuse (UWF and Herb Abraham) and aggravated assault (New Jack). Although DSOTR does display the darker side of the squared circle, it is balanced by the emotive stories of the families and wrestlers who knew the individuals covered and credit must be given to the creators for the way they have depicted the human side of each performer.

In the 1980s a documentary series such as DSOTR would've been inconceivable to fathom, when keeping the illusion that wrestling was not predetermined was paramount. Today, there is without doubt an innate fascination on the inner workings of the business. With the WWE's extensive catalogue of original documentaries, including *24*, *365* and *Chronicles*, fans have a plethora of material to dissect on the

Network. Away from the WWE umbrella there have been fascinating pieces over the past 25 years, which have enabled fans to get behind the curtain and infiltrate the once impenetrable kayfabe bubble.

It was a long-held industry creed from the earliest matches of the 20th century that keeping the notion that wrestling fights were 'real' was absolutely integral. Exposing the inner workings of the business was categorised as treason, with breaking kayfabe seen as the ultimate sin. Doing so would often see you physically beaten and unwelcome back into the business permanently. Feuding babyface and heel wrestlers were forbidden from being seen together, would not ride together and were to stay apart at airports in an attempt to emphasise the reality of the feud and to not expose the truth that they were not the characters they portrayed on TV. 'Hacksaw' Jim Duggan and the Iron Sheik didn't get this memo and they were famously pulled over by the police in 1987. The men were feuding in the ring at the time and thus should have been maintaining kayfabe and keeping their distance. The bigger problem for Vince McMahon was not the weed and cocaine they found in the car, but the fact that both men had been publicly shown to be socialising whilst in the midst of an angle. A reaction that, in the post wellness policy world, seems almost unimaginable. Duggan was let go by the WWF, although he was eventually brought back after the situation had cooled down.

In May 1996, ironically at MSG (the scene of the David Schultz incident) the kayfabe curtain was opened further for fans with the infamous 'Curtain Call' incident. This time it would be in front of a live crowd, secretly filmed by teenage buddies Jason Cosmides and Mani Mohtadi, who had smuggled a camera into the arena. A small action taken by two fans that would ultimately come to change the wrestling landscape forever. At the end of the main event that night the Kliq of Shawn Michaels, Triple H, Scott Hall and Kevin Nash openly embraced in front of the sell-out MSG crowd. Kevin Nash and Scott Hall were leaving to go to WCW. The problem was that the four men were feuding at the time and were seen to be breaking kayfabe by embracing so publicly in front of the sell-out crowd. The fundamental issue was that a large proportion of the backstage agents and wrestlers did not empathise with the emotional farewell. Backstage, Jim Cornette threw his suitcase down the hallway in disgust as he believed that the four men had spat all over the lineage of wrestling. By breaking kayfabe, the Kliq were seen by the majority to be tarnishing the legacy of those who came before them. The reality is that the live crowd loved the emotional embrace and the Curtain Call became one of the first viral wrestling videos of its kind on the fledgling internet. When Shawn Michaels and Triple H formed D-Generation X in 1997 the incident was referenced in an angle involving Vince McMahon. Whilst Vince looked visibly uncomfortable as the MSG recording played on Raw, the reality was that wrestling was now blurring the line between reality and fiction. The fans were hankering to know more about what went on behind the curtain and so were documentary filmmakers.

In 1996 Paul Jay began to film Bret 'The Hitman' Hart, following the Canadian for a calendar year. The documentary entitled, *Hitman Hart: Wrestling with Shadows*, gave a close-up perspective on what was to be the Hitman's last year with the WWF. Vince McMahon even gave permission for filming to take place at ringside and backstage throughout the whole process. A landmark moment in wrestling documentaries, Jay focused on how matches were constructed and 'called', with Pat Patterson openly discussing with the Hart Foundation how their match at In Your House: Canadian Stampede would go down. Patterson was seen disclosing intricate details about the booking of the fabulous main event, with the addition of the finish and what the story of the match would be. His words played over the top of highlights of the main event and it was a fascinating insight into match construction. This being permitted by the very same company that apparently fired a talent for breaking kayfabe just a decade earlier cannot be seen as anything less than an astronomical change of policy.

Of course, the central story of the documentary became the infamous Montreal Screwjob. Jay and his crew were at ringside for the biggest real-life double-cross in wrestling history. Bret, who was leaving WWF for WCW, did not want to drop the WWF Championship to Shawn Michaels in his home country of Canada (also his final PPV for the company before leaving for WCW), after Shawn had told him to his face that he would never put him over. Bret saw this as total disrespect and refused to drop the belt to Michaels in Montreal. As Jay's documentary reached its dramatic finale, the cameras would be there to witness the shocking conclusion to the Bret Vs Shawn feud in the Survivor Series '97 main event. Vince ordered the bell to be rung as Shawn placed Bret in the Sharpshooter, ensuring Hart did not leave Survivor Series with the WWF Championship and take it to WCW. The audio of Bret, *"They [WWF] screwed me, they really screwed me the lousy bastards"* played over the image of a broken Hitman, who was struggling to comprehend how 14 years of hard work and loyalty had become forgotten in an instant.

In 2020 we all know wrestling is predetermined, they are performers acting out their spots, promos and doing their 'jobs'. But at Survivor Series '97 in Montreal, the camera was firmly focused on the very real betrayal of a boss on his employee. As WWF often does so well, they reacted to a set of unplanned circumstances and astoundingly turned it into an overall net positive. The Mr McMahon character was born, and wrestling was more real than it ever had been. Bret states in Wrestling with Shadows, *"People say wrestling isn't real...it's a lot more real than you think"*. The documentary showcases the morality play of wrestling and suggests that the business is about far more than just who wins and who loses. It is about the individual, their passions, personal integrity and belief systems. The film allows fans to understand much more about a wrestler as a person and their personal motives. Beyond kayfabe you see the real-life personality which encompasses a huge part of Hart's in-ring persona. The Hitman character was more than just a job for Bret, he embodied it and what comes across is Bret's obvious battle to distinguish himself from his Hitman character away from the ring.

As a documentary piece *Wrestling With Shadows* resonates with wrestling fans, due to Bret's passion to keep the kayfabe persona of his character alive. A strange contradiction when you consider the purpose of the documentary was to achieve the exact opposite. The lines of kayfabe were blurred for the fans between Bret the wrestler and Bret the man. The majority of fans knew that Vince McMahon ran the WWF. However, they did not fully comprehend the extent that the Machiavellian owner would go to, to ensure the WWF Championship did not turn up on WCW Nitro. Paul Jay had inadvertently handed WWF their most compelling, believable and unbeatable heel ever. That was the man that owned the entire company, Mr McMahon.

In 1997, long time wrestling fan Barry W. Blaustein began travelling around America developing *Beyond the Mat*. He was attempting to understand the mindset of the men who would willingly choose to be professional wrestlers. When the documentary project began, WWF and McMahon were very much on board. Vince originally allowed Blaustein full access, but later tried to renege on the deal. Most suspect this was due to the depiction of self-mutilation in the documentary, with one wrestler going into intricate details on 'blading', a practice where wrestlers would use small razor blades to produce on-screen blood.

The documentary follows wrestlers at different points of

their wrestling journey. Terry Funk at the end of his career (or so we thought), Mick Foley during his WWF apex and a broken-down Jake 'The Snake' Roberts fighting on the indies for scraps. The film garnered positive reviews for the way it humanised the wrestlers behind the camera but didn't shy away from controversial issues, especially in the case of Roberts, depicting the impact that drink and drugs has had on his personal relationships. This story was also clearly the inspiration for Randy 'The Ram' Robinson in the critically acclaimed 2009 Hollywood hit 'The Wrestler' by Darren Aronofsky. A movie which bought the realities of what really goes on 'behind the curtain' to an even wider mainstream audience. The full extent of Jake's difficulties is brilliantly captured further in the redemptive 2015 documentary *The Resurrection of Jake 'The Snake' Roberts*.

WWF did not want to associate itself with Beyond the Mat after they realised the company (and wrestling) would not be shown in the most positive light. References to Robert's drug abuse, and the graphic depiction of violence in the film painted a picture of an industry that was mired in controversy. What Beyond the Mat does successfully is to convey how different wrestler's lives are to the average person. Humanisation is the key to personal identification, and the film certainly connotes the human side of what it is like to be a professional wrestler. The mental struggles; the try-outs; retirements; living on the road; being away from family, all irreparably changes the life of a wrestler.

Beyond the Mat sensationalises moments, but it also showcases the reality of what is like to be a wrestler outside of the kayfabe bubble. It may not be the most narratively consistent documentary, but it emotively illustrates the true pain of being a professional wrestler and the unfathomable lengths that performers will go to in order to 'get over' with a crowd and their peers. *"Close your eyes!"* shouts a stricken Collette Foley to her children as her husband Mick Foley is battered mercifully 12 times in the head with a steel chair by future Hollywood megastar Dwayne 'The Rock' Johnson. Why was Foley so willing to do this? To quote Oliver Reed in Ridley Scott's Gladiator, *"Win the crowd and you will win your freedom!"* The kayfabe envelope was opened further, as Foley is being stitched up backstage by WWF medics. He tells his young daughter Noelle *"It is just a little boo-boo."* The reality is that he has a severe concussion from the dozen chair shots and has little recollection of how the match concluded. Once again, events that do not play well in a post-wellness policy and concussion protocol industry.

With all of the documentaries referenced, kayfabe has now become almost obsolete. In 2020 most fans know wrestling isn't real, it is choreographed entertainment and we openly acknowledge the booker chooses who wins and who loses. Yes, there are countries such as India and Pakistan where the kayfabe bubble hasn't entirely burst but even they have a large and growing audience of 'smart fans'. The question is, does this deeper understanding lower our enjoyment when we watch? Wrestling over the past 20 years has become a medium obsessed with exposing the truth to its followers, rather than maintaining the façade of kayfabe. Wrestlers, on a daily basis now, engage in social media character wars on Twitter and Instagram to further their current storylines. The importance of social media has meant that the element of surprise is all but dead, with comebacks announced on The Bump or on a social media platform.

Kayfabe, the once sacred mandate of all wrestlers and bookers is now passé, as is the element of shoot style promos, filtered down by the micromanaged WWE script system. AEW has thankfully let its wrestlers have some more creative control with promos, which has led to some excitingly organic moments, with young superstars like MJF being allowed to thrive in the open playing field. As with all things relating to taste, some love wrestling's new direction and others (such as Jim Cornette) detest it. A reaction that isn't at all new to pro wrestling. In fact, it is often the exact same reaction that wrestling as an overall art form receives from the wider mainstream - deep appreciation or utter contempt. Why should the way that this art form is now presented be any different?

Fast forward to 2020 and the man that many considered the last beacon of kayfabe, The Undertaker. 'The Dead Man' allowed full access to the WWE documentary crew for a five-episode retrospective on his career and his final three years in the industry. A standout series for the company, primarily due to the Taker's frank honesty. The last outlaw of kayfabe, a man who has been notorious for keeping the truth of his character alive for 30 years bares his soul in a fascinating look at his home life, injuries and his fight for that one final perfect match. The running theme apparent in all of the documentaries discussed have been honesty and sacrifice with Mark Calaway openly admitting throughout The Last Ride that he is "chasing the dragon" for that last great match before he figuratively rides off into the sunset.

The Undertaker is not the only former world champion who has allowed his life to be intricately documented. Actor-turned-wrestler David Arquette opens up in the recently released You Cannot Kill David Arquette. Unlike Taker, Arquette's goal with the documentary is to brush off the tag of wrestling's biggest joke, after his infamous WCW title run in 2000. I applaud him for his transparency and quest to silence his wrestling critics. With vulnerable fragility he connotes a desire to change the perception that he dese-crated the lineage of the WCW Championship, externalising his real passion for the wrestling business. To the likes of traditionalists such as Jim Cornette, there is presumably nothing that can achieve this end. Any poster child for the breaking of kayfabe will likely forever be held on their wrestling blacklist - much as the kayfabe transgressors of the past would have been decades ago. Yet those traditionalists have now become the very tiny exception and no longer the overarching rule.

To the traditionalists who desired we cling to kayfabe forever the question best posed isn't "has breaking it made wrestling less enjoyable?" but rather "what other option did wrestling really have?". With so many other industries and sectors now being subject to full and open transparency, how could wrestling have honestly expected to stand alone as the exception? In short, it couldn't and it didn't.

The wrestling documentary has certainly evolved our perspective of professional wrestlers over the past 25 years, and much like The Undertaker himself, kayfabe has become past its prime. The wrestling documentary and the reliance on social media has allowed fans behind the curtain to see the real-life personalities behind the characters they admire. In our social media centric society it is very difficult to imagine a return to a kayfabe world where performers stay apart in fear of breaking the illusion of their feud. The old way of kayfabe has been corrupted by the changing technology of the wider world, with wrestlers now unable to get away with their transgressions on the road without it being recorded on a passing fan's iPhone. Knowledge is seen as power and in the wrestling world backstage, knowledge has allowed fans to view their favourite performer as much more than just someone who falls through tables or lands on thumbtacks. They are humans who have the capacity to feel real pain, they are fathers and mothers who regularly miss their children's birthdays. As Blaustein says so pointedly in Beyond the Mat, *"They're just like you and me, except they're really different!"* With so much backstage knowledge now available kayfabe has been unable to survive and like many of our favourite wrestlers kayfabe has sadly had to retire. But unlike a wrestling retirement, this retirement is for real!

. . .

BOX OUT: MUST SEE WRESTLING DOCUMENTARIES

Wrestling with Shadows (1998) Documentary filmmaker Paul Jay goes into fabulous detail about the tumultuous last year of Bret Hart's tenure in the WWF.

Beyond the Mat (1999) A close-up insight on why people would willingly choose to be a professional wrestler. Features Mick Foley, Terry Funk and Jake Roberts.

Undertaker: The Last Ride (2020) A five-chapter journey delving into the Deadman's career and final three years in the WWE.

"30 for 30" Nature Boy (2017) A fabulous biographical feature on Ric Flair. Goes in depth into his career, infidelity and his jet-flying lifestyle, which made him such an iconic figure.

The Sheik (2014) Former WWF champion gives an unprecedented look at his upbringing in Iran and how he became one of America's greatest wrestling villains.

Louis Theroux's Weird Weekends: Wrestling (1999) British documentary legend Louis Theroux throws himself in at the deep end, as he delves into American professional wrestling. He encounters 'Sarge' on an infamous WCW try-out as his new persona, 'Waldo'.

Andrè the Giant (2018) A TV produced documentary on the French 'Eighth Wonder of the World'. Varied talking heads with Dave Meltzer, Hulk Hogan and an emotional Tim White (Andre's handler).

You Cannot Kill David Arquette (2020) Filmed over three years, chronicling the actor and former WCW champion's desire to not be seen as a wrestling joke.

The Resurrection of Jake 'The Snake' Roberts (2015) Witness DDP try to turn the life around of his wrestling inspiration. A battle to help Jake exorcise his demons.

Dark Side of the Ring (2019-) Fantastically researched, the Benoit and Owen Hart episodes are thought provoking pieces and essential viewing. A real balanced perspective on the perils of being a professional wrestler.

THROWING AWAY THE RECEIPT

Issue 30, June 2021

Katarina Waters

After a UK wrestler ended up in court in March 2021 for giving his opponent 'a receipt' during a show, Katarina Waters took a closer look at wrestling's dubious history with accepted and violent revenge inside the squared circle. She also assessed how the fallout from this case has the very real potential to change pro wrestling forever.

The Scout Hut on Cherry Grove in Ferndown, Dorset, England is the last place that most would expect as the site of one of the most important wrestling stories of the decade, if not ever. Yet on Saturday February 8th 2020, that's exactly what it became. British wrestler 'Jiving' Jay Knox (33) was performing a match in front of a relatively small handful of fans, against trainee wrestler and his own student, Rob Wilson (32). Wilson, returning to wrestling after a long absence, was drafted into the contest last minute, after Knox's original opponent was unable to make the event. Despite initial apprehensions, Wilson agreed for the match to be 'called in the ring', after his opponent and trainer assured him it would be fine. The only call of importance to our story, however, is the one that Knox made out loud, several minutes before the bout's conclusion. The call wasn't an overly complex string of words, instructing the inexperienced Wilson to run, jump, duck or move. Rather, it was comprised of just two syllables, intended to issue a warning of what the less experienced man was about to receive. The word didn't proclaim a manoeuvre, but rather a historic and well-known wrestling concept. Uttered under Knox's breath, the word was short and to the point - "*receipt*". Within seconds of saying it, Knox (real name James Riley) sprung to his feet and kicked Wilson extremely hard in the face. The consequences for both men would ultimately be catastrophic.

Wilson was unable to shield himself from the blow and the tremendous force of the kick was apparent to almost everyone sat in attendance. Yet it wasn't until Wilson's face became visible once again that the severity of the damage it had caused became known to all - including to the man who had induced it. Within seconds, the ring filled with blood. Onlookers shouted for the contest to be stopped, while children in the audience cried. As Wilson himself would go on to say, "*my face just exploded, and I realised it was a lot more than a broken nose*". His diagnosis was sadly correct. After still finishing the match, Wilson was helped backstage, where he later collapsed. It wouldn't be until he was taken to hospital that Wilson, a married father of two, gradually began to understand the full extent of his injuries. He had suffered a fractured jaw, eye socket, nose, and teeth.

As regular as injuries are in pro wrestling, it's not until you view video footage of the kick, alongside a picture of Wilson's face in the hospital shortly afterwards, that you could truly begin to understand the seriousness of what had happened. So serious in fact, that when Wilson's family called the police, James Riley (Knox) was subsequently charged with a criminal offence. Upon further review of the evidence, Bournemouth police believed that they had enough to present the case to the Crown Prosecution Service, in the hopes of a trial. The CPS agreed that the evidence was sufficient, and a tentative date was set at Bournemouth Crown Court. The result of that trial and the precedent that it might set, should Knox have been found guilty, instantly transformed the incident into something else entirely. It was now something that had the potential to affect every single person within the wrestling industry globally. Just like that, a contest between two unknowns of 'professional' wrestling, taking place in front of virtually no audience, and in a venue likely never heard of by all but a handful of fans, was about to become one of the single most important showdowns in British wrestling history - at least from a legal perspective.

You don't have to be a historian of the sport to know that 'receipts' are a fairly normal and regular part of pro wrestling. Unlike other shady elements of the industry, such as drug use and sexual misconduct, the receipt has been far less hidden from the eyes of prying fans. Over the years, many a receipt has taken place on global television, even on Pay-Per-Views and the issue has eventually become the subject of podcasts and full-length documentaries. In fact, Vice's 'Dark Side of the Ring' gave a sizable portion of their episode about New Jack to the story of how he allegedly intended to murder Vic Grimes during a scaffold match - as a receipt for a botched spot, years earlier, in ECW. Although, this being pro wrestling, rather than the attempted homicide being the basis of a lawsuit or prison sentence, it instead became one of the more viral examples of this somewhat accepted wrestling custom. So why was the case of Rob Wilson and James Riley so different? There were two main reasons. Firstly, because this time the police looked at the incident for what it was - intentional, grievous bodily harm, along with compelling video and photographic evidence to prove it. Secondly, it was different because Wilson, unlike so many others before him, wasn't afraid to press charges for fear of what it might do to his career prospects as a pro wrestler. When presented in the cold light of day, and with the overwhelmingly visceral conse-quences of Riley's actions clear for all to see, this case was not simply about a 'silly wrestling tradition gone too far', but rather a serious, criminal act. Proving so in court, however, was going to be an entirely different challenge altogether. After all, one doesn't have to search very far to see a path that could feasibly lead to Riley's ultimate defence.

While it would be both unfair and unwise to speculate as to whether or not Vince McMahon kept certain employees under contract to serve as 'enforcers', there is certainly enough evidence to imply that the industry leader at least knew about receipts taking place as a part of their in-ring business. This was more visible during 'The Attitude Era' than ever before. Certain talents such as JBL and Bob Holly were engaged in some awfully unprofessional incidents. Incidents that were not too far removed from that which transpired between Wilson and Riley.

JBL's seemingly unprovoked assault on The Blue Meanie at the WWE-produced 'One Night Stand' Pay-Per-View has become the stuff of legend. The resulting bloody injuries to Meanie actually fit the textbook description of GBH. How about Bob Holly's assault on the since-passed Tough Enough contestant Matt Cappotelli? Again, an assault that led to similar injuries to those which were received by Wilson, at least visually. Also, much like Riley, this saw Holly in the role as 'trainer' too. Again, the battering of Cappotelli was broadcast on television and the narrative quickly transformed from 'should Holly be fined, suspended, fired or even arrested' into 'was Cappotelli really cut out for the business?' As shocking as these incidents were, for both Holly and JBL (much like New Jack) they were not isolated one-off events. Rather, they are highlighted as 'notable mentions' in a long series of 'receipts' which they'd served out to trusting opponents both before and since. Regardless of any speculation as to whether WWE higher-ups sanctioned these 'lessons' or not, it can surely be argued that they allowed them to happen again and again, simply by not taking serious action against those responsible. Both Holly and Bradshaw remained in employment for many years afterwards, and in some ways, the incidents only served to add to their on-screen and backstage reputations.

When such high-level on-camera assaults are not only aired but go unpunished, at least in any meaningful way, there is bound to be an eventual industry fallout. For example, it would make sense for younger wrestlers watching on to assume such actions were an accepted part of the top tier wrestling business they aspired to be in - and then to emulate them. It could therefore also have been put forward by Riley's defence council, that Wilson should have been forewarned of the many-decades-long tradition of 'receipts'- and thus to claim such a thing was now GBH would be inaccurate. After all, it wouldn't be the first time that the on-screen actions of WWE/F wrestlers were used as a legal defence, and not just for assault either. Just over twenty years ago, they were even utilised as a defence for cold-blooded murder.

THE DEFENCE

When a then twelve-year-old boy by the name of Lionel Tate was arrested for the murder of six-year-old Tiffany Eunick in July of 1999, the case made worldwide headlines. Yet those headlines centred less on the tragic death of the victim and far more on the proposed legal defence put forward by Tate's lawyer, James Lewis. Eunick's horrific list of injuries included a lacerated liver, broken ribs, and a fractured skull. These came as the result of Tate lifting her into the air and smashing her tiny body onto a table in his living room. Taking place at the height of the Attitude Era, the defence for the murder was simple - Tate had merely been replicating the actions of his heroes in the World Wrestling Federation. In other words, it was 'play wrestling' gone terribly wrong. Calling the strategy a *"contrived hoax"*, the WWF likely desired to be as far away from the incident as possible. Why wouldn't they? Their new, edgy product was already under fire from some sections of the media, who claimed that it was poisoning the minds of America's young. WWF getting involved in the trial almost certainly wouldn't have made a difference either way. The jury of ten women and two men found Tate guilty of first-degree murder after just three hours of deliberation - an incredibly short time considering the nature of the case.

Along with his defence, his sentence was equally historic too. Tate, age 13 by the time of sentencing, would become the youngest US citizen to ever receive life in prison without the possibility of parole. Despite the defence strategy clearly not working, in January 2002 the state appeals court overturned the conviction on the basis that Tate's mental competency had not been evaluated before trial. He was subsequently released on one year's house arrest and a ten-year probation. He would violate the terms of his house arrest just seven months later, being found outside carrying an eight-inch knife. Then, just eight months after that, Tate was charged with armed burglary with battery, armed robbery, and violation of parole. He is not expected to be out of prison until just before 2050.

While it seems evident that in the case of Lionel Tate the 'wrestling defence' was a mere smokescreen to cover up the actions of a deeply troubled young man, it's debatable that it could be employed somewhat more effectively in the trial of Jay Knox. After all, the incident happened not to a six-year-old child in somebody's house, but inside of a wrestling ring on a ticketed event. As a result, physical contact and some form of perceived violence, albeit simulated, is mutually consented to. Especially considering that the pair had agreed to hit each other with hardcore weapons, which are often used at full force without 'pulling' the shots. This could illustrate that certain parts of the match would already be 'stiffer' than others, as decided on by both combatants in advance.

Then, there was the offending kick itself. Had Wilson, who was kneeling at the time, been more upright in his position, the kick would not have connected with his face, but rather across the chest. Such a kick is commonplace in pro wrestling nowadays, traded in strong style match sequences all the time. Additionally, by current standards, these types of kicks are more often than not delivered with incredible force, even when pre-agreed. After becoming a staple of Japan, such kicks were made famous in the US by Low Ki in Ring of Honor. They were then adopted all over the industry by high-level performers like Samoa Joe and CM Punk, eventually making it all the way to the WWE, becoming a signature of Daniel Bryan. Could it be put forward in court that Knox had intended to perform such a kick to the chest, but in his angry haste and due to Wilson being out of position, the kick landed on his opponent's face instead? If so, how could a jury with zero wrestling experience be equipped to differentiate between a misplaced kick to the chest and intentional GBH instead? Surely, if such a defence was to be used, pro wrestling would be able to provide hundreds, if not thousands of examples of this very thing being an accepted 'spot' in pro wrestling. Thus, Wilson could conceivably be framed as the one at fault in the incident, purely for not being 'in position' quick enough when it landed. When Knox eventually was interviewed under caution by the police, he did indeed claim that the kick in question was aimed at Wilson's chest, making the prosecution's case considerably trickier in the process. The plot thickened.

The increase of 'stiffness' of strikes within the squared circle has unquestionably been on a steep incline over recent decades. Once only seen on the indies, 'strong style wrestling' was slowly assimilated by the American mainstream - first, courtesy of Impact and then the WWE. Many of the former top stars of companies like ROH would go on to become headliners for the industry leader, and with them came the more physical style that they'd made their early names with. This change in style would induce a lasting effect upon audience tastes too, increasing fan expectations for hard hitting action across the board. As a result, it created an on-screen product where the fine line between intentionally 'stiffing your opponent' and just 'working snug' became more blurred than ever before. So much so, that should James Riley's defence council decide to pursue the notion that this was just 'snug working gone awry', the prosecution would likely have a hard time convincing a jury that the victim could have had no idea what to expect, physically, in a modern wrestling match. To wrestling insiders now looking in on this bizarre situation, the story was a truly fascinating one. For at its heart wasn't just the trial of James Riley. In no small way, it was simultaneously the trial of the entire industry of professional wrestling, along with the extreme consequences of its modern-day style and historic backstage culture.

In spite of the monumental nature of the case few, if any, wrestling journalists or personalities appeared aware of it, at least prior to its court date. This was strange considering how earth-shattering any conviction against Riley could turn out to be for the business at large. Unlike wrestling news, in legal news often less emphasis is placed on by day-to-day convictions, and more on landmark rulings. Such rulings, where a 'legal first' takes place, are fundamentally important because they set precedent. In common law legal systems, such as the UK's, a precedent is a legal case that establishes a new principle or rule. This is then used by the courts or other judicial bodies when deciding later cases with similar issues or facts. In short, using precedent allows a level of predictability when examining potential cases that fall into the same or similar category, giving those involved a better idea of what a verdict might look like ahead of time. This encourages solicitors representing clients who have been the victim of a comparable offence to pursue legal action. Equally, it enables both police and prosecutors to feel that their time might not be wasted in court when taking further action. In the most basic terms, a conviction against Riley would set a legal precedent that could result in major implications for everyone in pro wrestling. The stakes were extremely high.

STUCK IN ITS WAYS

Whilst all this was going on, the receipt continued to be a commonplace trope of the wider business. Yes, COVID-19 might have meant an end to almost all live shows, yet YouTube and podcasts filled the void, with wrestlers openly joking with opponents who had previously given them receipts in the past. Eric Bishoff's 'mean tweet receipts' segment became a regular part of his fantastic 83 Weeks show, where the former head of Ted Turner's WCW would verbally assault those who'd been mean to him on Twitter. In fact, in recent years the receipt had gone from being an industry secret to an open one. In 2021 it has now finally become something altogether different entirely - a meme! Is it any wonder that such an environment could induce something the likes of what transpired at a tiny Scout hut in Dorset?

The fact that the accused even mouthed the word "receipt" at his victim prior to the assault further serves to illustrate the detachment from reality that wrestling suffers from. Not only does it suffer from it, but it arguably relies upon this detachment in order to exist in the first place. Almost as if telling an 'in joke', where the punch line is a real punch, wrestling has created an environment where such actions are just 'a rib' or a 'loving lesson'. Like a parallel universe, seemingly existing outside the rules and regulations of a civilised society, wrestling was finally about to wake up from this illusionary, split reality. The industry was imminently about to stand trial, and not in 'wrestlers court' this time, but a real one. Would the day-to-day occurrences of a business free from governing bodies and outside intervention prove its continued right to stand free of further scrutiny? Or would the untamed environment which the sport had always been, finally be proven as an outdated, unregulated beast, ready to be put out to pasture? Now, as a consequence of failing to implement a proper professional body of any description, wrestling would be unable to defend itself. Its fate would instead rest in the hands of solicitors, the jury, and a judge.

There is a philosophical argument that has often been made to justify the receipt. It's also the argument used to explain away the hazing of new talent. The argument has been that it's all about proving younger talent 'respect the business' or convincing veterans that rookies care for the well-being of their opponents. The theory is that if you hurt someone (almost always accidentally), you deserve to get hurt back in order to learn a lesson. Alongside that is the view that if you don't respect the business, often, you then damage it and thus hurt your co-workers in another way - financially.

Regardless of if these justifications ever had merit or not, the reality is that their existence was often less about teaching valuable lessons to younger talent and more about retaining a power dynamic over them. It would typically be the older veteran that decided when it was fair or just to dish out a physical reprimanding. This opened the door to systemic abuse; and, as was proven by the likes of JBL and Bob Holly, being a repeat offender of such misconduct yourself didn't mean that you too were liable for the same type of abuse in return. Rather, they were celebrated as 'tough guys' and pushed with gimmicks that actually created entertainment out of their unprofessional actions. Using one's own greater level of power and higher social standing to inflict violence against someone with far less, and to do so with zero fear of consequences, has another name. It's called bullying! As CM Punk mocked in his infamous 'pipe bomb' promo on June 27th, 2011, the WWE's 'Be A Star' anti-bullying campaign could be accused of vast hypocrisy when the past actions of Holly, JBL and the like are given further review.

To lay this problem solely at WWE's feet, however, would be greatly unfair. Especially as some of the most dangerous (and questionably criminal) examples of receipts happened elsewhere. As mentioned, the New Jack/Vic Grimes incident took place in Rob Black's XPW. Prior to this, Jack (real name Jerome Young) was tried on charges of assault and battery with a dangerous weapon after slicing open the head of wrestler Mass Transit (17) on an ECW house show on November 23 rd 1996. At the request of Transit (real name Eric Kulas), Young agreed to 'blade' him in order to have blood in their match. Deciding to teach the youngster a lesson, Young cut too deep and severed two arteries in the rookie's forehead, leading to severe blood loss before Kulas passed out. When the incident finally made it to court, some three years after it took place, Young was acquitted of all charges in the criminal trial and later declared not liable in the civil one. The fact that Kulas had lied about his age and experience didn't help his case. Even though the courts decided in New Jack's favour, one need only look at some of Young's other actions in the years to follow, along with his own words regarding them, to conclude that his intentions inside the ring were not always what some might consider 'within the law'. Yet, despite this, he continued to be booked in the business for almost two decades since, doubling down on his dubious actions multiple times in the process. Many within the business, or so it appears at least, simply turned a blind eye. As far as 'receipts' being a criminal offence, the

Mass Transit incident provided clear precedent to the contrary, legally speaking at least. Ethically and morally? Well, that's something else entirely.

The tale of Mass Transit is so well known by almost all within the business, that it's fair to speculate on the lasting consequences of it. The 'not guilty' verdict unquestionably paints a picture of wrestling as a lawless yet complex industry, that the courts are simply unqualified to correctly assess - no matter how graphic the nature of the violence! Therefore, it implies that even something as serious as that which happened to Eric Kulas is still 'fair game' in the eyes of a judge and jury, not just to those in the business. After all, this is the same industry where Bruiser Brody was murdered in a dressing room - in part, as a consequence of his past 'stiffing'. What's more, no one has ever been found guilty or punished for it, despite many in the industry claiming to know who committed the crime. Worse still, that person continued to wrestle in Puerto Rico's WWC, where the stabbing of Brody occurred, for many years afterwards. Clearly, an industry has severe issues when serious assault, attempted murder and actual homicide result in no real-world consequences or loss of employment for those involved. Perhaps Rob Wilson and the Crown Prosecution Service had now become an unwitting instrument of justice for the crimes of pro wrestling's murky past? Not viewing Riley's 'receipt' through the same rose-tinted glasses as so many institutionalised wrestlers, Detective Constable Steve Davis of Bournemouth CID summed up the incident clearly. *"James Riley subjected his victim to a violent assault that went far beyond anything that was appropriate within the parameters of the wrestling match. The victim has been left with injuries that have had a significant and lasting impact"*. Both men's fate, along with that of wrestling as a whole, now awaited to see if the British legal system agreed with DC Davis's assessment. After some delay, a trial date was finally agreed for the 25th of February 2021.

VITAL VERDICT

As with most epic wrestling dramas, this one wasn't without its own unexpected swerve. In a shocking, last minute twist, Riley changed his plea to 'guilty' just before the trial could begin. Perhaps Riley hoped for a suspended sentence by changing his plea and saving the CPS time and money at a trial? Although, if this was his hope, to do so in the very final moments prior was likely not viewed favourably by many. Least of all Wilson, who had already undergone several facial surgeries, was now suffering from PTSD, and had lost his job as a consequence of the assault. It was a financial blow that was deepened considerably since his new found unemployment occurred just before the onset of the pandemic and government lockdowns. For Wilson to be dragged through the additional burden of a year long pre-trial process was undoubtedly further stress for him as well as those close to him. Something which could have been avoided had Riley changed his plea many months earlier.

On Monday, March 29th, 2021, James Riley was sentenced to 21 months in prison after admitting to inflicting grievous bodily harm upon Rob Wilson. The judge also imposed a ten-year restraining order against Riley, preventing him from contacting either Wilson or his family. For one of the first times in history, actions that took place in-ring were forcibly ejected from the bubble of pro wrestling and analysed by institutions outside of it. It was concluded that what pro wrestling considers to be 'just part of the business' was, in fact, criminal in the eyes of UK law. Perhaps any legal defence used by Riley would have been undone by him admitting to the assault in text messages to Wilson in the days that followed their match. In one exchange, Riley confessed to his victim "*I acted like an animal*", claiming that one of Wilson's own kicks earlier in the match had "*lit him up like a Christmas tree*". It was an invariably poor excuse for what Wilson would go on to suffer as a consequence. Additionally, another witness who spoke to the police told a similar story of being punched in the face by Riley for real in a match prior to his bout with Wilson.

With all factors taken into consideration, it is clear that Riley was the one at fault in relation to this incident. However, the circumstances which allowed such an incident to happen in the first place may be far more nuanced. With the previous assaults on Eric Kulas, Matt Cappotelli, The Blue Meanie, Vic Grimes, Bruiser Broody and a catalogue of others having seemingly gone unpunished, and the use of strong style kicks now being more commonplace than ever, Riley could perhaps even be seen by some as a victim himself. Pro wrestling's past and a lack of action from those in power to eradicate this type of accepted behaviour created a situation where something like this wasn't just possible - it was inevitable. Now, two young men's lives have been irreparably damaged because of a culture of normalised assaults, which has been passed down through generations of grapplers and often allowed by their employers. With this landmark case, there may finally be a forced change taking place.

Just over one week after the sentencing of Riley, British Wrestling's new All-Party Parliamentary Group published their 100-page report regarding the safeguarding of British wrestling's future and the well-being of those involved. Almost like a one-two punch for the UK scene when combined with the Riley/Wilson case, the British establishment has finally taken the inner workings of pro-wrestling seriously. Of course, despite previous failed attempts to spark such interest in the nation's lawmakers and institutions, this increased focus on the industry's inner workings was finally set in motion - for very good reason. Namely, the result of the

Speaking Out movement in the summer of last year. This movement shone a much-needed light on another form of systemic abuse within the wrestling business, this time sexual in nature. The fact that this has all happened in a very similar time period as the Wilson/Riley court case is purely one of life's strange coincidences. Now, the potential real-world consequences of such actions are finally being made manifest for the entire world to see. Perhaps wrestling is invariably receiving a receipt all of its own?

While it's great that new eyes are finally investigating some of wrestling's outdated practices, it would be unfair to claim that many within the business weren't already waking up to the changes that needed to be made. On August 26th 2017 AAA wrestler Sexy Star gave a famous 'receipt' to Rosemary at the company's TripleMania XXV event, seemingly attempting to break her opponent's arm in the shocking fiasco. For one of the first times in recent memory, both fans and insiders spoke out publicly against Star, with many calling for her to be blackballed. In multiple cases, she was. This included Cody Rhodes making it clear that she would never set foot in one of his locker rooms. This was a major turnaround for an industry which had by and large viewed such assaults as just par for the course in the years prior. Now, in part due to social media, anger at those who engage in such conduct has rapidly become far more audible. With this in mind, it would be nice to conclude that at least some of those in pro wrestling can be considered responsible enough to have a guiding hand in deciding the industry's long-term future. For that to happen, however, those currently holding power need to do something that they've long struggled to achieve - they must finally learn to work together! Failure to do so could see any power which they currently possess swiftly be taken by others more willing to drag professional wrestling forwards. Just this time with far more emphasis put on the 'professional' part of the equation.

And what of WWE's role in all of this? Well, after decades of adopting what can best be described as an isolationist attitude towards anything which occurs outside of their own company, this business worldview may need to be drastically changed. Likely changed sooner rather than later, that is. For in the coming years the 'industry leader' could come to find that, unless the affirmative action required to truly live up to that title is taken, the industry, with help from the politicians and unions, might just lead itself somewhere else altogether. While some might view both Rob Wilson and even James Riley as sacrificial lambs, laid at the altar as an offering for wrestling's past sins, it could be wise to look upon them in a different way entirely. Their story and the consequences that it has had and will continue to have for both men, make them more like canaries in the proverbial coal mine. As the canary was used for alerting miners to the presence of dangerous gases, these two men now provide a stark warning of their own. A warning which is long overdue in an industry that has been leaking toxic gas for far too long. If their cautionary song is acknowledged, others might just avoid the same fate. If it is ignored, however, this case could just be the first of many more like it in the years to come.

WrestleTalk Magazine would like to thank the victim, Robert Wilson, for his co-operation with us for this article. We applaud his bravery for standing up and pursuing official action.

SMOKE WITHOUT FIRE

Issue 52, November 2023

Dee Adams

The glitz of professional wrestling hides a shadowy past, from the National Wrestling Alliance's 1950s FBI investigation to the mysterious death of Dino Bravo. In this article, Dee Adams uncovers the sport's ties to organized crime, including its intricate connections with the Yakuza, revealing a side of wrestling rarely discussed in the spotlight.

If you're reading this then I suspect you already know that professional wrestling has always been a bit, well, dodgy. In fact, it's been very dodgy. From Bruiser Brody's backstage murder to the cocaine train that was the 80s and 90s, professional wrestling has often appeared to exist in its own lawless bubble, separate from the rules and consequences of 'normal' society. Sure, over recent years a concerted effort has been made to 'clean up' the business (on a surface level, at least) but watch any shoot interview with any old timer and you will be regaled with stories of GBH, drug abuse, sexual harassment, blackmail and extortion. Perhaps more shocking than the stories themselves is how we, the fans, and the wrestlers in question are so desensitised to them. These stories are the product of bygone glory days and are often examined through a haze of nostalgia instead of the criminal lens they truly deserve.

Taking this into consideration, I thought writing an essay on the history of organised crime within professional wrestling would be easy. It turns out I was wrong. Whilst there is indeed a lot of smoke, it has proven quite difficult to locate the fire (with the exception of professional wrestling in Japan - more on that later!) Either the crimes committed weren't very well organised, or they were _too_ well organised and left little in the way of a paper trail. One thing was clear, and that was that most 'big-time' promoters have undoubtedly had to call in favours from influential friends over the years. Some of those friends were in Congress but others... well, let's just say they probably operated at a more 'local' level.

So, now what? Due to a 'lack of evidence' (remember that phrase - you'll be hearing it more later) I can't very well start accusing folk of having ties to the mob. I don't want to be sued. Or killed. However, what I can do is present you with my findings and allow you to come to your own conclusions. So without further ado, let's get stuck in.

THE NATIONAL WRESTLING...CARTEL?

According to the Oxford English Dictionary, a cartel is "*an association of manufacturers or suppliers with the purpose of maintaining prices at a high level and restricting competition.*" In the United States of America, cartel behaviour is considered a criminal violation of antitrust laws, with offenders at risk of paying high fines and perhaps even jail time. This is due to the belief that cartels cheat consumers and other businesses. They attempt to increase members' profits while maintaining the illusion of competition.

But what does that have to do with professional wrestling? Well, on 18th July 1948, the National Wrestling Alliance was formed. The NWA was a governing body for a group of regional professional wrestling promotions. The group operated a territory system. Each promotion had its own champions whilst simultaneously recognising a singular world champion who would travel around defending his title. The different promotions partook in talent exchanges and would work together to protect their territorial integrity and effectively freeze out those who weren't under the NWA banner.

It wasn't long before the NWA caught the attention of the FBI who noted that it was essentially operating as a cartel. In October of 1956, the National Wrestling Alliance was brought before the Justice Department for violating antitrust laws. Fortunately for the NWA, one of its founders, St. Louis-based promoter Sam Muchnick, was a very well-connected man. During World War II he served in the Panama Canal Zone alongside a man called Mel Price. Price would go on to become chairman of the House Armed Services Committee and would use his power and influence to help negotiate a consent decree. This decree allowed the NWA to continue without doing much to change any of its anti-competitive, mafia-like practices.

Not only did Sam Muchnick have friends in high places, he had them in low ones too. He was a known associate of Al Capone as well as Hollywood actress and gangster's moll, Mae West. Despite his proximity to the mob, Muchnick was adamant that he had nothing to do with them, nor did professional wrestling. In an interview with Roy D. Hunter of the Department of Justice, Muchnick would say; *"We, in the wrestling business, have prided ourselves through the years that we have kept our game clean from outside influences and, unlike other sports, we do not have thugs or gangsters connected to it."*

Now while there is nothing on record to say that the mob

were involved in professional wrestling in the same way that they were boxing, they certainly were fans of the sport and could often be seen at ringside. In his autobiography, *Listen, You Pencil-Neck Geeks,* Freddie Blassie talks about wrestling the legendary Bruno Sammartino in New York. On this particular night, he defeated Sammartino by kicking him in the balls and having him counted out. This was back when kayfabe was still in full effect, and the crowd was furious. After the match, Blassie mistakenly found himself in Sammartino's dressing room. Sammartino, still selling the nut shot, was stretchered into the room surrounded by hangers-on. Blassie wrote, "*In every town, the most powerful Italians latched themselves onto Sammartino and decided that they were his protectors - whether Bruno wanted them there or not. Some of these guys were business-men, others were political types, and a few - I'm sure - were mobsters. I'm not implying for a second that Bruno would ever have any deal-ings with the Mafia on his own. But he'd gotten so famous that he couldn't always pick the boneheads who chose to band around him.*" The two men couldn't break character in front of all the hangers-on, so Blassie shouted, "Look at that! Typical Italian stunt! You hit him in the neck, and he grabs his balls." At that, Jilly Rizzo, a close friend of Frank Sinatra with ties to the mob, pulled out his gun and threatened to kill Blassie. A quick-thinking Sammartino, still in character, defused the situation by saying, "No, let him go... I want him for myself the next time we step into the ring." Kayfabe almost cost Blassie his life, but it saved him as well.

Blassie wasn't the only wrestler to get on the wrong side of the mob. Early in his career, Captain Lou Albano teamed with Tony Altomore to form The Scillians. As a tag team, the two men portrayed themselves as stereotypical Italian-Amer-ican gangsters, complete with fedoras and black gloves. They wrestled primarily in Chicago and were even able to win the NWA Midwest Tag Team Championships in June 1961. Unfortunately, the local Mafia was unfamiliar with the term 'imitation is the sincerest form of flattery' and a message was passed on to Albano telling him to cease his portrayal of a mafioso, as it was embarrassing and disrespectful. The Sicilian gimmick was quickly dropped, and Albano and Altomore left Chicago and moved onto another territory just to be on the safe side.

Due to the secretive nature of both professional wrestling and the mob, it will be difficult to prove how much crossover there ever was. Muchnick's claims that the mob was in no way connected to the business may seem a little naive to some. Perhaps his territory of St Louis truly was gangster-free but it's unlikely the same can be said for others. The mob has notoriously gravitated to where the money was coming in and back then professional wrestling was doing huge numbers. This combined with the fact that professional wrestling was a relatively unsanctioned industry full of morally dubious characters, would've made it an ideal venture for crime bosses across the country. Unfortunately, we'll probably never know the scale of their involvement for sure.

SHADY SECOND JOBS

Modern day professional wrestling is often referred to as a morality play - an eternal battle between good and evil. Nowhere is this more prevalent than in Mexico, where Lucha Libre, through its técnicos (heroes) and rudos (villains), tells a narrative that reflects societal values, ethics, and the age-old human struggle between right and wrong. Through its colourful pageantry and symbolic storytelling, Lucha Libre transcends mere entertainment, offering a mirror to society and a reflection on the complexities of morality. From the El Santos movies of the 1960s to Místico declaring his support for the National Action Party (PAN) during the 2009 elections and urging people to support them in the fight against drug trafficking, Lucha Libre has always stayed on the right side of morality. Publicly, at least. That's why it was so shocking on 28th August 2022 when Mexican independent wrestling promotion Promociones Freseros Brothers cancelled their show due to two of their luchadors being found dead.

Earlier that week, the remains of Salvador Garcia, who wrestled as Lepra Mx, were found in plastic bags in the neighbourhood of La Lupita in the north-central state of Guanajuato. A few days later, the body of Raul Salazar Santillan, who wrestled as Maremoto, was found dumped behind a National Guard barracks in the city of Irapuato. Both men had jobs in the local government (Santillan as a drainage worker and Garcia as the coordinator of inspectors of the Directorate of Markets of the municipal presidency) but this isn't what got them killed. A banner was found near one of the bodies written by the Jalisco New Generation Cartel (CJNG), in which they claimed responsibility for the bodies and accused the deceased of being part of the Santa Rosa de Lima gang. Both games have been fighting turf battles against each other in Guanajuato for years. The murders were 100% gang related and the Jalisco Cartel made a point of making sure that was known. "*To the colleagues of the Lucha Libre profession, the CJNG has nothing against you personally,*" the banner found by one of the bodies read. "*The events involving " Juventud Rebelde 'Jerry', Lepra Salvador and Maremoto were direct attacks.*"

While the local wrestling community was no doubt saddened by the passing of their fellow luchadors, one can only imagine the sense of relief they felt at hearing the CJNG publicly declare that they had no vendetta against the Lucha Libre profession. The Jalisco New Generation Cartel is considered by the Mexican government to be the most dangerous criminal organisation in the country. It is heavily militarised and notoriously much more violent than other cartels. The cartel has also been noted for cannibalising some of its victims as well as using drones and rocket-propelled grenades to attack its enemies. Definitely not the kind of people you'd want to get on the wrong side of, as Santillan and Garcia so tragically found out.

Unfortunately, they weren't the only professional wrestlers to get involved in organised crime and lose their lives for it. On 10th Match, 1993, Adolfo Bresciano, better known as Dino Bravo was found dead in his living room, having been shot 11 times. He was 44 years old.

Born in Campobasso, Italy, in 1948, Bravo emigrated to Canada with his parents when he was young, settling in Montreal. He began wrestling in the 1970s and quickly found great success as Canada's hottest young wrestling star. Though Bravo was initially against the WWF's monopolisation of the wrestling industry, Vince McMahon eventually made him a financial offer he couldn't refuse and he ended up signing with the company in 1986.

For the next few years, Bravo enjoyed a lucrative career in the WWF, earning hundreds of thousands of dollars a year. While he wasn't always satisfied with his job and how he was booked, Bravo was more than satisfied with the luxurious lifestyle afforded him by his WWF paycheck. He put a down-payment on a big house in a well-to-do Montreal suburb, bought several nice cars, and developed a penchant for designer things. However, in 1992, Bravo was released from his WWF contract. Having been a wrestler his whole adult life, Bravo was now in the unenviable position of having to start over from scratch, and unfortunately entry-level jobs that would allow him to maintain his lifestyle were pretty much non-existent. Legitimate jobs, at least...

The Cotroni crime family, based in Montreal, Quebec, were a formidable organized crime syndicate with roots tracing back to the 1920s. Founded by Vincenzo 'Vic'

Cotroni, who immigrated to Montreal in 1924, the family quickly established its influence in the criminal underworld. Over the years, they engaged in various illicit activities, drawing the attention of law enforcement agencies, including the United States Federal Bureau of Investigation (FBI), which considered them an extension of the renowned Bonanno crime family of New York. Dino Bravo was actually related to the Cotroni family - his aunt was married to Vic. For years, Bravo made a point of steering clear of the Cotroni family's dodgy dealings. His former tag-partner Rick Martel recalled him once saying, "*I know I could go into crime and make really good money, but I don't want to go that route. I know myself, and I know what kind of guy I am...*" But as Bravo's debts mounted he became more and more desperate until he could no longer resist the lure of the Cotroni family. He began to work for his uncle as a driver and debt collector/enforcer. He would then go on to take part in an illegal cigarette smuggling scheme.

Illegal cigarette smuggling, often referred to as "cigarette trafficking," involves the illicit transportation, distribution, and sale of cigarettes without paying the appropriate taxes or in violation of tax laws. This activity is driven by the potential for significant profits due to the price differences between jurisdictions with high and low cigarette taxes. Dino Bravo quickly learned how lucrative this business could be, especially if her leveraged his fame.

The local indigenous people controlled the river and were able to ship in all kinds of contraband. They also happened to be huge wrestling fans and were more than happy to work with *the* Dino Bravo. With the help of the indigenous people, Bravo's cigarette smuggling venture began to thrive and it wasn't long until others began to take note. He was approached by cocaine smugglers who said they would let him in on their deals if he let them in on his. Bravo agreed, unaware that this would lead to his downfall.

In early 1993, Bravo stored $400,000 worth of illegal substances in a warehouse in the belief that one of the cocaine smugglers whom he'd been working with would pick it up. The shipment had been there for three days when the cocaine smuggler came to pick it up, only to discover police had raided the warehouse. The cocaine smuggler was furious, blaming Bravo for the costly blunder. Bravo, however, was adamant that the cocaine smuggler was at fault and that he should have picked up the shipment sooner. What had looked to be a lucrative business deal had turned very, very sour.

On the evening of 10th March 1993, Dino Bravo's wife, Diane, left their house to take their young daughter to ballet class. When she returned a little before midnight her husband was dead, having been shot eleven times. He was still sitting in his armchair with the TV remote in hand and the television was still playing. There were no signs of a struggle or forced entry. In fact, beyond the very obvious fact that Bravo had been murdered, there were no signs that anyone had been there at all.

Police were never able to find Bravo's murderer but their investigation did draw a few chilling conclusions. It is widely believed that Dino Bravo knew his killers. He clearly let them into his home and felt relaxed in their presence, hence why when he was found he was still sat in his armchair with the TV on. Police hypothesised that whoever was responsible for his death had probably gone to his home under the guise of watching hockey with him. Based on Bravo's loose grip on the TV remote, police believe he was shot from behind, caught completely unaware. If he had known he was about to be shot, his body and subsequently his grip would've automatically tensed up, which wasn't the case. The bullets found at the scene were traced back to two guns, heavily implying that there was more than one killer in the house.

So who killed Dino Bravo? The truth is that nobody

knows. Police were unable to trace the killers but many believe that his death was a result of his involvement in organised crime. Everyone who knew him has a theory. Some believe it was the cocaine dealers with whom he'd had a falling out. Others believe that he may have run afoul of the indigenous people who'd helped him set up his cigarette smuggling scheme. It's even been suggested that his death could've been at the hands of the Cotroni family, though some of those closest to him seem to think their theory holds less weight. Whatever happened, one thing is clear; Dino Bravo thought he was in the company of friends, and whoever it was betrayed him in the most violent, final way possible.

PURORESU AND THE YAKUZA

"I shall pay the damage with my life. That's what I've been thinking all this time. Showing with my action...It's the only way I can compensate myself." These chilling words can be found on the final page of *Bankruptcy! FMW,* the book-cum-suicide-note of former FMW owner and CEO, Shoichi Arai. His body was found hanging from a tree in Tokyo's Mizumoto Park at 6:20am on the 16th May 2002. He was 36 years old and around $2,340,000 in debt.

Arai hoped that his life insurance payout combined with the sales of his book would be enough to clear the debts he'd accrued since taking control of Frontier Martial-Arts Wrestling in 1995, a promotion so hardcore it made ECW look like your Granny's bingo night. The company had made massive financial losses during its last few years due to a combination of embezzlement, incompetence, and sheer bad luck. Not only did they have to weather the 1997-1998 Asian financial crisis, they lost their TV deal, ticket sales plummeted, and, in what would be the tragic final nail in the coffin, the company's top star, Hayabusa, was injured during a match and left permanently paralysed from the neck down. The company was haemorrhaging money and Arai, desperate to pay his wrestlers and keep his promotion afloat, ended up seeking help from Yakuza-affiliated loan sharks. These loan sharks charged extortionate amounts of interest (30% for 10 days) and Arai quickly found himself having to borrow more money from different sharks in order to pay off his existing loans. This quickly spiralled and it wasn't long until his debts reached the millions.

According to Japanese law, using a closed place to question somebody is regarded as 'imprisonment' so a lot of loan sharks choose to do their interrogations in public places. On 14th February 2002, Arai found himself cornered in a Tokyo cafe, surrounded by ten sharply dressed thugs who wanted to know when and how he was going to pay them. Upon hearing that he had no money, they demanded he sell the FMW ring but to their disappointment discovered it was utterly worthless because 'no one wanted to buy it'. His home had already been seized by the bank and he'd sold his car to try and clear some debt. All Shoichi Arai had was a 1000 yen note in his wallet - around $10. He then got a phone call from one of his employees from the FMW office, telling him that it was surrounded by loan sharks. At this point, Arai knew it was over and so he began to concoct his life insurance scheme. Three months later he was dead. Unfortunately, the money from his insurance policy didn't cover all of his debts and his family was left to pay them for years after his passing.

As shocking as Shoichi Arai's story is, it's not altogether surprising. The Yakuza's involvement in Puroresu (The Japanese loan word for professional wrestling) has always been something of an open secret. Countless 'gaijin' wrestlers have spoken about their experiences with 'sponsors' and 'the men in suits who always sat in the front row'. In his autobiography *Pure Dynamite,* 'The Dynamite Kid' Tom Billington recalls being backstage at a show and witnessing an intense confrontation between wrestling legend Antonio Inoki and a Yazuka member; *"They were speaking in Japanese, so I don't know what they were saying, but at the end of it, Inoki bowed and the man slapped him right in front of all the other Japanese wrestlers. Inoki said "Domo arigato." Well, I knew what that meant...he had just thanked the Mafia man for slapping him across the face. That's true."*

The Yakuza have been involved in Puroresu ever since Rikidōzan introduced the sport to Japan in 1953. Rikidōzan, who is often called 'The Father of Puroresu' was closely affiliated with the Yakuza, if not an acting member himself. Depending on whose accounts you read, he was either a wonderful man, worthy of his legacy as a Japanese sporting legend, or a low-down, dirty thug who built his empire – wrestling promotions, nightclubs, hotels, condominiums, and even a golf course – on the suffering of others. What we do know for sure is that in December of 1963, Rikidōzan was murdered in a Japanese nightclub by Yakuza member Katsushi Murata. The two men got into an altercation which ended up with Murata stabbing Rikidōzan in the stomach. He succumbed to his injuries a week later and Murata ended up spending several years in jail. Upon being released from jail Murata would go on to become a high-ranking member of the Yakuza, but he never forgot Rikidōzan. Every year, on the anniversary of his death, Murata visited Rikidōzan's grave to pay his respects right until his own passing in 2013.

So what ties the Yakuza so strongly to Puroresu? Chris Jericho, who himself enjoyed many tours of Japan during the 1990s, wrote in his 2007 book *A Lion's Tale: Around the World in Spandex* that he believed the Yakuza laundered money via ticket sales. He's most likely right. The Yakuza have been operating in Japan since 1612 and have grown to become "the biggest private equity firm in the country." They operate their businesses through thousands of seemingly legitimate front companies to hide their illicit proceeds within legal industries such as the construction, real estate, and finance sectors. The professional wrestling companies that received Yakuza backing were most likely fronts for far more sinister activities.

In 2012, the Yakuza bubble well and truly popped on the Japanese wrestling scene. Pro Wrestling NOAH, the early 2000s darling of the professional wrestling world, had experienced a rough few years. In 2009, Mitsuharu Misawa, the founder and top star of the company, tragically died mid-ring during a tag match. In the years that followed, they lost their TV deal due to the recession and crowd numbers dwindled dramatically. In 2004 they'd managed to sell out the 55,000-capacity Tokyo Dome, and now they were struggling to draw more than a thousand fans to a show. Pro Wrestling NOAH's future was looking more and more uncertain with each passing week. In response to this, the promotion decided to make talent cuts to save money and several wrestlers were released. One of the wrestlers, Jun Izumida, decided not to go quietly and released a book exposing Pro Wrestling NOAH's ties to the Yakuza. In his book, he named NOAH executives Ryu Nakata and Haruka Eigen as alleged Yakuza associates and claimed they had a role in Misawa's widow being swindled out of $250,000. He even went as far as to assert that many of NOAH's top stars were sponsored by the Yakuza and would often attend parties at gang members' homes.

The fall-out was almost the final nail in the coffin for the once mighty Pro Wrestling NOAH. Nakata and Eigen swiftly stepped down from their management positions. The company released a statement saying that they were going to create some new compliance regulations and courses to educate their wrestlers and employees about the perils of organised crime to ensure that nothing like this happened again. Although the company tried to distance themselves from the scandal as much as possible, the damage had already been done. TV companies didn't want to work with Yakuza-associated businesses and it has taken them almost ten years to repair their reputation.

Over the past few decades, the Yazuka has been romanticised by western media, and many have found themselves fascinated by their code of honour and their unique sense of chivalry. People like to talk about how the Yazuka were among the first on scene to help after the 2011 tsunami and some even credit them with keeping the crime rate in Japan so low. But for every story showing the Yakuza in a heroic light, there are many more featuring people like FMW's Shoichi Arai. The Yakuza make the bulk of their money from things like gambling, extortion, brothels, drugs, and people trafficking. Their presence in the Puroresu scene should never have been a welcome one.

HE SAID-SHE SAID AND THE TRUTH IN BETWEEN

While researching this article, I was shocked at the number of stories I came across alleging serious wrongdoings within and around the professional wrestling industry. From tales of bribery and corruption to drug use and murder, it seems as though there is very little that hardened veterans of the industry haven't witnessed at some point in time. However, it is worth noting that professional wrestlers are storytellers both by trade and nature. There is no way of knowing how accurate their recollections are or whether they've been embellished over the years. Memories aren't as reliable as many like to think; they can be manipulated and distorted, influenced by external factors. Whilst there is rarely smoke without fire, there is almost no evidence to prove that many of the crimes that allegedly took place within the professional wrestling bubble actually happened. Considering the industry was built on secrecy, this lack of evidence is hardly a surprise. It serves as neither an admission of guilt nor proof of innocence. That being said, the fact these tales of lawlessness and debauchery were so widely and readily accepted (and in some cases even lauded and admired!) should surely give cause for alarm.

For better and for worse, professional wrestling is a business like no other. It's a world in which the extraordinary becomes the norm and often it attracts larger-than-life characters, both inside the ring and out. It's a world that has managed to be loud and brash on the surface whilst being shadowy and secretive underneath. The journey through the murky waters of wrestling's entanglements with organised crime leaves us with more questions than revelations, a dance of smoke and mirrors where the line between legality and criminality is as blurred as the line between performance and reality. Professional wrestling has always been notoriously protective of the secrets that shroud it and it's probably safe to say that we'll never know the full extent of the industry's ties to organised crime.

Ultimately, one can only hope that today's wrestling professionals have taken heed of the clouded past and learned from the mistakes of their predecessors, steering clear of the shadows of organised crime. May they chart a path that honours the sport's legacy while distancing themselves from the shadows of its checkered history.

ABOUT THE AUTHORS

ABOUT WRESTLETALK

WrestleTalk is the world's biggest wrestling media brand, with over 1 million YouTube subscribers and around 8 million monthly video views across its main and sister channels. The WrestleTalk.com website is now the most viewed news site in the industry, generating around one hundred million page views annually. On top of this, the brand has expanded into various other areas, including the bi-monthly WrestleTalk Magazine (from which the articles in this book are taken), live events, and online merchandise store WrestleShop.com. Collectively these elements provide wrestling fans across the globe with all the news, entertainment and insight they need to get their full fix of the professional wrestling world.

ABOUT THE AUTHORS

Oli Davis first took over as the lead producer of WrestleTalk's YouTube channel at the start of 2016, having previously worked in production and live broadcast transmission for Channel 4, Bauer Media, ESPN, BT Sport and NBCU. As well as being a hugely popular on-air personality, he has overseen the brand's growth into multiple new areas such as podcasts, live events, broadcast television shows, live-streaming, print media, merchandise and WrestleTalk.com, which is now among the biggest wrestling news websites on the planet.

A lifelong wrestling fan, Dave Bradshaw has spent over 15 years as a play-by-play commentator and become one of the most recognisable voices in independent wrestling worldwide. He is also an NCTJ-trained journalist who regularly writes features for WrestleTalk Magazine and is currently preparing to author his first book. He has previously reported news for national and local media and also has experience working in the UK Parliament and in the higher education sector. Now working full time for WrestleTalk, he divides his time between writing content, developing new projects and coordinating the creative output across our channels.

Adam Pearson is a British actor, presenter, and campaigner. Since childhood he has suffered from neurofibromatosis, a genetic condition that causes non-cancerous tumours to grow along nerves, Pearson has faced challenges throughout his life. However, he has turned these challenges into opportunities, advocating for disability rights and raising awareness about the condition. A vocal advocate, Pearson has spoken out against bullying and discrimination. He has also been involved in various charitable endeavours, working to change perceptions and promote understanding of people with visible differences.

Katarina Waters has spent almost 20 years working in the content and entertainment industry. Formerly a high level female wrestler, Kat moved to America in 2006 where she would go on to wrestle for the WWE and other large American companies. After showcasing her work for multiple major television networks across the globe, Kat transitioned into acting work appearing in several movies and TV shows. It was during this time that she began writing and producing her own content from her home base of Los Angeles. With almost two decades of experience, she provides insight into the wrestling world from a truly unique perspective.

Dee Adams is a passionate writer with a deep-rooted love for professional wrestling. A lifelong wrestling enthusiast, Dee's fervour for the sport is evident in her contributions to WrestleTalk Magazine, where she delves into the intricate world of wrestling, offering insights, reviews, and analyses. Beyond her wrestling commentary, Dee is an accomplished author, having already published two books with several more on the way.

THE MOST CRITICALLY ACCLAIMED
MAGAZINE IN WRESTLING

PRE ORDER YOUR COPY NOW
THE SEQUEL TO THE MOST CONTROVERSIAL WRESTLING BOOK OF THE YEAR
WRESTLETALK
PRESENTS
THE
FALL OUT
VS
WWE AEW
THE SHOCKING SEQUEL TO 'THE NEW WAR'
WRESTLING'S NEW WAR REACHES A NUCLEAR CLIMAX
ALSO AVAILABLE ON
amazonkindle
COMING SOON
WWW.WRESTLESHOP.COM

Made in the USA
Monee, IL
05 July 2024

61311111R00105